The Filipino Fighting Whip

The Filipino Fighting Whip

Advanced Training Methods and Combat Applications

Tom Meadows

Foreword by Dan Inosanto

Paladin Press • Boulder, Colorado

The Filipino Fighting Whip:
Advanced Training Methods and Combat Applications
by Tom Meadows

ISBN 10: 1-58160-477-7
ISBN 13: 978-1-58160-477-1
Printed in the United States of America

Published by Paladin Press, a division of
Paladin Enterprises, Inc.
Gunbarrel Tech Center
7077 Winchester Circle
Boulder, Colorado 80301 USA
+1.303.443.7250

Direct inquiries and/or orders to the above address.

Cover photo by Scott St.Clair

Visit our Web site at: www.paladin-press.com

This book is dedicated to Frank and Frances Stearns. Their yard was always a haven I could go and play in when the other neighbors would say, "Tommy, why don't you take that whip and go play somewhere else?"

Tom Meadows and Frank Stearns in 1959.

WARNING

The techniques presented in this book are dangerous and should not be practiced without the supervision of an authorized, qualified instructor.

There are few weapons that can injure or maim you as severely as a whip. I highly recommend wearing full safety gear, but be aware that you can still be injured even while wearing such gear.

Training with the whip requires aerobic endurance, and I strongly recommend that you consult with a physician before attempting any techniques shown in this text.

The author, publisher, and distributors of this book disclaim any liability from any damage that a reader or user of the information contained in this book may incur. This book is *for academic study only.*

Contents

Foreword

It is an honor and a privilege to write this foreword for Tom Meadows' new book. Tom has studied the martial arts at my Academy since the 1980s and has gone on to distinguish himself by placing first in the superheavyweight division in the first World Eskrima Kali Arnis Federation (WEFAF) International World Championship Eskrima tournament. Tom has continued his martial arts training, studying in Doce Pares eskrima and receiving instructor status under Grandmaster Cacoy Canete.

Not all Filipino martial arts systems use flexible weapons, such as the whip, but those systems that do, have designed uses for such items as the headband, scarf, bandanna, sash, rope, belt, chain, *olisi toyuk* (nunchaku), sarong, malong, and whips of various lengths.

In LaCoste's System of kali, eskrima, kuntaw-silat, and bersilat, a system in which I have had the privilege of training with Juanito (John) LaCoste, the whip is rarely used alone and is usually supported by an additional weapon, such as the stick, staff, or dagger.

I have also had the privilege of training in the whip in the Sayoc system of kali, under Mike Sayoc. My instructor and friend, John DeJong, also taught me the whip system from the Indonesian art of pentjak silat.

Tom's studies, research, and experimentation in the use of the whip led him to develop his own version of whip training. His insights are a welcome addition to the martial arts community.

Dan Inosanto, Founder/Head Instructor
Inosanto Academy of Martial Arts
Los Angeles, California

Tom Meadows (left) with Dan Inosanto .

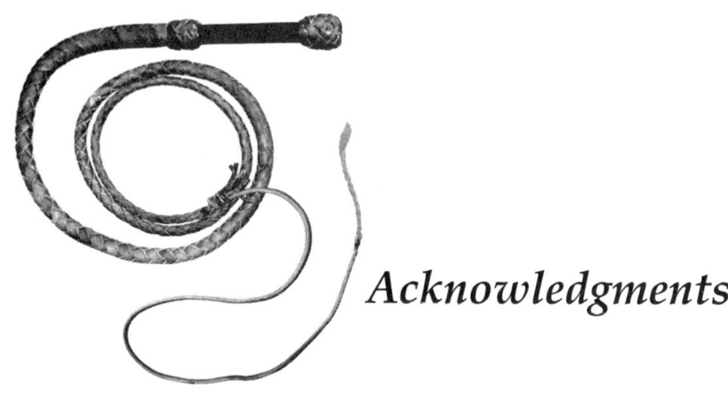

Acknowledgments

It is impossible to write a book all by yourself. Whether it is the person who made the typewriter or the supplier of ink for your fountain pen, there is always someone to whom you are indebted in your creative process.

When I look at the text of this book, there are many faces and names that come to mind. The first person I always think of is Frank Stearns. Frank took great pleasure in having a 5-year-old kid come over to his house and trim the dandelions with his bullwhip.

I also think of a man I met in 1963, a mestizo who worked at a motel we were staying in on Route 66 in Arizona. I sneaked out of my parents' room at 6:00 A.M. to play with my whip, and he came over to me, hung a napkin on the stairwell, and taught me the overhand crack. He didn't speak English, but we both spoke the universal language of the whip.

Thirty years later, I found another mentor for the whip, Guro Dan Inosanto. While all the other students at the Inosanto Academy were playing with their sticks and knives,

I had found Guro Dan's collection of whips that he kept in the weapons cabinet. The whip is a fundamentally antisocial weapon, which meant that I had to practice out in the parking lot of the academy. While I was doing this, another academy student, Anthony DeLongis, came out to watch and coach me. In the short space of half an hour, he showed me a level of technical excellence that started me on a 15-year path of study and ultimately led to this text. I still train with Anthony to this day and consider him one of the finest whip instructors in the world.

As my growth in the Filipino martial arts continued, I came across many people who encouraged my growth and development in the whip arts: Steve Grody, my Jeet Kune Do tutor in the early years; Ted Lucay-Lucay; and the members of the Dog Brother's community—each in their own ways strongly influenced my approach to the whip.

My continuing path in these arts brought me in contact with others who carried the legacy of the whip: Sam Tendencia, who used his Filipino *hilot* to heal my joint displacements and body misalignments, was also a long-term practitioner of the whip arts. As my training progressed, I found that Momoy, Diony, and Cacoy Canete had all been involved in developing whip techniques in the Doce Pares system for the past 50 years. I am particularly indebted to Grandmaster Cacoy for our personal training together over the past 15 years.

There are also the people who cross the boundaries of friend, instructor, and mentor: Mike Krivka, my first student of the whip, and Guro Jeff Finder of Serrada fame. In addition, Simo Paula Inosanto, Jeff Wolcott, Barry Smith, Steve Best, Brian Ader, Professor Ron Lew, Ron Balicki, Steve Kohn, Sifu Ted Sotello, and especially Chris Smith have each contributed to my development as a whip stylist in some critical way.

Special thanks go to James Loriega for his advice and support, which greatly added to this book; Mark Ward for technical editing and review; and Paladin Press editor Jon Ford for his patience and guidance.

Finally, I have to offer special thanks to Marian Castenado, who published my first article in *Martial Arts Training* magazine. When I told her about my whip work she said, "You really ought to write a book about that," and so I did.

To each of these people, I offer my thanks and my appreciation for their contribution to this work.

Tom Meadows
July 2005

Part One

HISTORY AND BACKGROUND

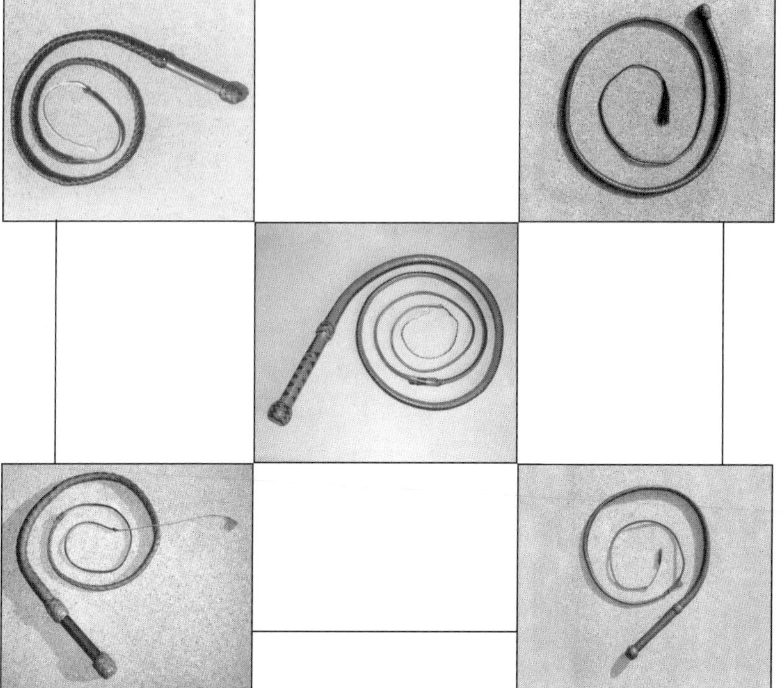

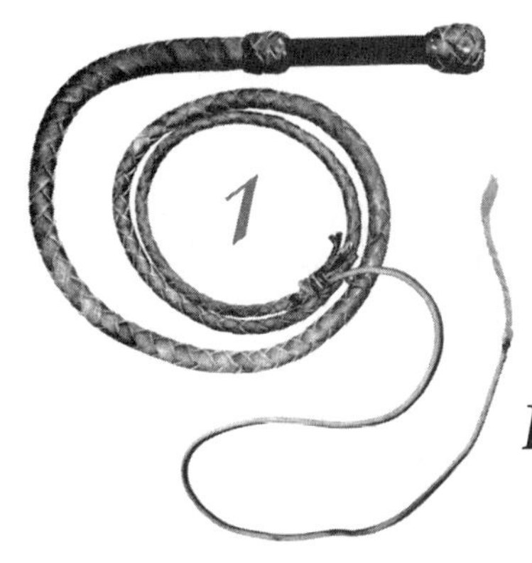

The History and Evolution of Filipino Whip Techniques

The whip is one of the oldest tools developed by our primitive ancestors. One unique aspect of the whip is that it is not specific to any one culture or time period, but is found in virtually all cultures on all continents. Examples have been found in most every ancient culture, including African tribesmen, Chinese rice farmers, and the highly developed Egyptians.

As man developed, he evolved from hunting and gathering to farming and harvesting grain. The harvesting led to the domestication of animals for food and labor for tilling the fields. This use of animals in agriculture created the need for new ways to control them, which led ultimately to the invention of the whip.

As a herding tool, the whip was essential because many animals have very tough hides and a high tolerance for pain. The whip allowed the herder to effectively gain the animal's attention from a safe distance. The whip also proved to be an effective tool in protecting the herds from predators.

With the development of whips that used physical impact to guide livestock came the sophistication of using the whip as a noisemaker. No one knows for sure, but the practical evolution of learning to crack a whip more than likely came from someone discovering that he could snap a piece of wet cloth or from observing small children playing with a vine or piece of bull kelp seaweed at the seashore. It could only have been a short step from these observations to experimenting with using the sound of the whip to control and direct animals.

Whip users in past centuries were primarily involved in animal husbandry. Both herdsman and drovers were judged by their ability to keep their animals healthy, under control, and protected from predators. This forced the development of refined whip techniques that caused no harm to the animals yet allowed precise control over a large herd.

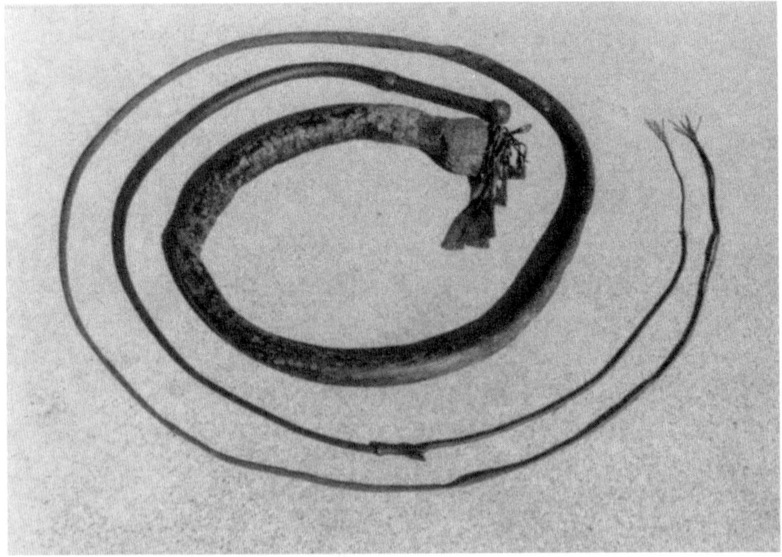

Bull kelp seaweed shown in direct contrast to a finely woven whip. Note how the taper of the whip closely matches the perfect natural taper of the seaweed. A piece of this seaweed will crack as powerfully as the most expensive whips but will disintegrate into many pieces after three or four cracks.

Contemporary whip practitioners are the recipients of this legacy of refinement and control. The European whip practitioners and the cowboys of America, Australia, and New Zealand have brought the arts of using and making the whip to an entirely new level.

The focus of this text is on this legacy of refinement and control. Although this legacy is critical to good whip handling, it is not enough in itself on which to build a combative foundation. This foundation must come from a culture that has extensively explored the combative use of the whip. Thus the material in this text isn't presented from the perspective of the Europeans or the cowboys, but instead from within the 1,500-year-old tradition of the Filipino martial arts.

ESKRIMA, ARNIS, AND KALI: THE FOUNDATION ARTS OF THE FILIPINO FIGHTING WHIP

Over the past 40 years the terms *eskrima, arnis,* and *kali* have become synonymous with the Filipino martial arts as a whole. These terms are also often used to refer to individual styles or specific branches of the Filipino martial family tree. The spellings of these terms can vary from style to style, typically to reflect the culture or heritage of a particular family or region.

I had the good fortune to begin my Filipino martial arts training under Guro Dan Inosanto when these arts were first coming into the prominence they enjoy today. When asked, "Which is better, eskrima, arnis, or kali?" Guro Inosanto replied: "Take everything you can get." This simple advice turned out to have profound, long-term implications that provided the spark for the research that led to this text.

In pursuit of Guro Inosanto's direction, I have trained with more than 35 instructors in the martial arts. The information presented here is intended to honor the technical foundation and culture as presented to me by each of these men and women. Thus, you will find the word *eskrima* used when referring to the Doce Pares system and the variant *escrima* used to refer to the Serrada system, since these are the spellings preferred by the men who created these systems. Other terms will also be found with several spellings, again to reflect the wishes of the practitioners of the various styles.

Language is intended to communicate information and, ultimately through this communication, to unify people of different cultures and lifestyles. The choice of language in this text is intended to simplify the presentation of the technical resources of the Filipino martial arts, honor all teachers of these arts, and provide a common training ground for students interested in these arts.

In this book, the term *eskrima* will be used to reflect styles that originate in the central Philippines, *arnis* for the arts originating in the northern part, and *kali* for the Moro styles of the southern Philippines. Each of these regions prefers a distinct group of weapons, and these preferences are different enough that they can be used as a positive indicator of a warrior's given style or region. The common ground shared by all these arts is that each uses the stick, the dagger, and the stick and dagger in combination as part of their core curriculum. These are considered the hallmark weapons of the arts of eskrima, arnis, and kali, and are what makes them distinctly Filipino in nature.

FILIPINO WHIP STYLES— THE FLEXIBLE WEAPONS OF INOSANTO-LACOSTE KALI AND DOCE PARES ESKRIMA

The technical foundation for the whip techniques in this book comes primarily from two systems of the Filipino martial arts: Inosanto-LaCoste Kali as taught by Guro Dan Inosanto and the close-range Doce Pares eskrima system of Grandmaster Cacoy Canete, which is known as his Corto method.

Guro Dan Inosanto trained with Bruce Lee for many years and is responsible for the integration of Filipino fighting tech-

Dan Inosanto at his academy in Marina Del Rey, California.

niques and martial concepts into Lee's fighting system. Guro Inosanto met his eskrima instructors through his father, Sebastian Inosanto, and ultimately trained with more than 26 men we today would classify as masters of the Filipino martial arts of eskrima, arnis, and kali.

One of these men, Juanito (John) LaCoste, had a very extensive training background, and he categorized his kali training into 12 areas, listed below. If you examine section nine, the flexible weapons, you can see that there are 10 weapons in this category. Guro Inosanto has inherited some very unique applications of these weapons through his training with John LaCoste and others, and these applications will be reflected in this book.

Weapon Categories of Inosanto LaCoste Kali

1. Single stick, single sword, single ax
2. Double stick, double sword, double ax
3. Short and long (*olisi-baraw*)
    a. stick and dagger
    b. sword and dagger
    c. sword and shield
    d. stick and shield
4. Double knives (*baraw-baraw*)

5. Knife and empty hand (*baraw-kamut*)
6. Pocket/palm sticks (*olisi-palad*)
7. Empty hands (*kamut-kamut*)
    a. kicking (*sikaran*), choking
    b. boxing (*panatukan, songab*)
    c. grappling/wrestling (*dumog*)
    d hit, tie and untie (*pitik-pitik*)
    e. pinching, biting
    f. finger thrusting (*hampak-higot, hubad-lubad*)
    g. elbow and knee
    h. finger flicking
8. Long weapons, staff, oars (*bankaw-sibat*)
9. Flexible weapons
    a. whip (*latigo*)
    b. stingray fishtail
    c. rice flail (*olisi-toyuk*)
    d. scarf or handkerchief (*panu*)
    e. jacket (*kanggan*)
    g. rope
    h. headband (*putong tagkus*)
    i. belt (*sabitan*)
    j. cloth around waist (sarong)
    k. Chain (*kadena*)
10. Throwing weapons
    a. sand
    b. coins
    c. mud
    d. yo-yo
    e. top
    f. dagger
    g. spikes
    h. rattan and bamboo darts
    i. spear
    j. light spear

11. Flying projectiles
    a. bow and arrow (*pana*)
    b. blowgun (*sumpit*)
    c. sling and slingshot
12. Mental, emotional, and spiritual training

Three of the weapons listed in section nine have a strong bearing on the study of the whip: the latigo whip, the stingray tail, and the olisi-toyuk, which is better known as the nunchaku.

The latigo whip refers specifically to a leather whip. It can be any type of leather whip, including bullwhips with short wooden handles, horse whips with very long handles, and the shorter riding crops.

The stingray tail seems to be unique to the Maphilindo (Malaysian-Philippino-Indonesian[1]) martial arts. Stingrays frequent shallow waters, are easy to catch on a baited line, and reach very large sizes. Their tails can easily grow to 30 inches in length and have a poison stinger, or telson, on the tip that can be up to 2 inches long. When the tail is removed and dried, it becomes leathery and semirigid, with a very coarse texture similar to rough sandpaper. A light hit with a stingray tail to any bare flesh will draw blood, and it was not unusual for the coarse skin to be coated with a poison. The stinger end tends to be a little fragile and usually breaks off on impact. The stick techniques of the Filipino martial arts transfer directly to the stingray tail, with the added benefit that the ray tail's flexibility allows it to curve over and around any blocks or weapons in its path.

The nunchaku are familiar to anyone who has seen a Bruce Lee movie, but few realize that the weapon he used, the olisi-toyuk, is found in the Philippines and that the techniques he displayed were from the Filipino martial arts.

---

1. Guro Inosanto coined the term *Maphilindo* before *Filipino* became the standardized spelling of *Philippino.*

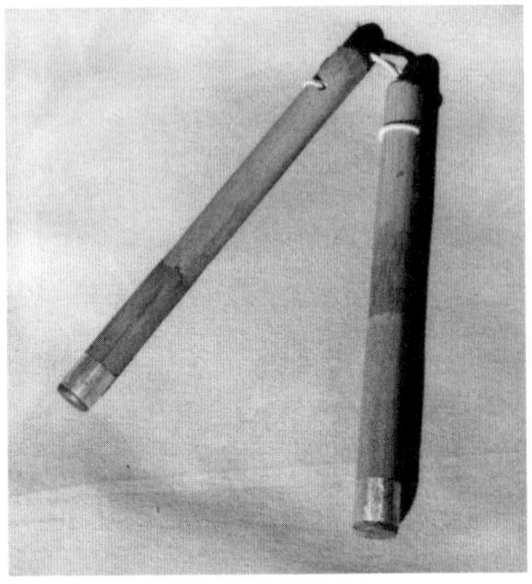

A Filipino olisi-toyuk. Note the rope connection, rather than the metal connection used in most of the Asian rice flails, or nunchaku. This rope connection is believed to allow faster spinning action.

Both the nunchaku and the olisi-toyuk have common roots. Both originated as farming tools designed to remove the hulls from rice. The Asian and Filipino cultures rely heavily on rice as a staple food, and field workers have always used some type of manual flail for removing the hulls. When bandits attacked the workers in the rice fields, the rice flail was always close at hand and easily employed as a weapon of self-defense. Thus, it has found its way into both the Filipino and Asian martial arts.

The Filipinos have a 1,500-year history of stick and blade training, and the olisi-toyuk was readily adaptable to this existing technical structure. The twirling movements of the olisi-toyuk are also directly applicable to short whip techniques, and studies in this weapon form an important part of advanced short-whip training methods.

WHIPS OF DOCE PARES ESKRIMA

Several types of whips are found within the Doce Pares eskrima system. The first type of whip is a 28-inch baton with an equal length of rope attached to one end and a short popper attached to the end of the rope. This is classified as a stock whip because of its handle length, and it can be used as a baton or whip, as well as a combination of both.

The second type of Doce Pares whip is the braided manila rope whip, as designed and used by Grandmaster Momoy Canete. This design closely parallels a contemporary Australian stock whip. Momoy used a unique swiveling attachment to connect the manila rope whip to its handle, and this led him to develop some interesting attack angles that can only be duplicated with a whip of this design. Rope whips are very powerful in their own right and, when properly constructed, can function as effectively as the latigo-type whips.

The primary focus of this text is on leather (latigo) fighting whips, which can be as short as 3 feet or as long as 6 feet. Whips longer than 6 feet are difficult to manipulate at close range and, as such, have limited combat effectiveness; therefore, they aren't covered in full detail here.

CONTINUING EVOLUTION OF FILIPINO WHIP TECHNIQUES

The flexible weapons examined in this text form an important part of the technical foundation of the whip as it is found in the Filipino martial arts. To understand the development of this foundation, it is important to realize that the Filipino combative arts have never stagnated, but rather have maintained continuous development throughout their 1,500-year history and that this process continues even to this day.

An example of this continued evolution is found in modern eskrima handgun disarms. One hundred and fifty years ago Filipino tribesmen did not spend their training time practicing handgun disarms; their primary focus was on the baton, the blade, and dance forms containing fighting movements.

However, with the occupation of the Philippines by the Japanese during World War II, the development of handgun disarms became necessary to survival, so they are now found in many contemporary eskrima systems.

The Filipino martial arts have applied this evolution to the centuries-long tradition of using flexible weapons, the whip in particular. These fighting arts, while noted for their extreme effectiveness, have always been characterized by movements that are both graceful and flowing. During the Spanish occupation of the Philippines, from roughly 1565–1898, combative training was outlawed, thus forcing the Filipinos to disguise their combative training in dance forms. This ultimately led to the development of the flowing movements that are seen in the contemporary Filipino martial arts.

One of the unique principles of the Filipino arts is that these fundamental flowing movements translate easily from weapon to weapon and to empty hands as well. The whip is no exception to this principle; by studying basic techniques used in the various Filipino martial arts, you can create a foundation of movement that applies directly to the whip.

Once the whip is taught from this standpoint of pure movement, a common ground is created for all whip practitioners, whether cowboy, theatrical performer, or combat stylist.

Although this text focuses on the whip as found in the Filipino martial arts, it also acknowledges the Western and Australian influences on these arts. The Filipinos fought with the Australians and the Americans in World War II, and this resulted in a technical exchange of fighting knowledge, including whip techniques. This contribution to the Filipino martial arts is reflected in contemporary Filipino whip work.

LATIGO Y DAGA WHIP TRAINING METHOD

The continuous technical evolution of the Filipino martial arts is the direct by-product of the ongoing process referred to by

Guro Inosanto as "uncovery." In truth, no one invents or discovers a new technique in the Filipino martial arts; rather, through training or exploring new facets, practitioners find movements or physical techniques that are new to them. More than likely, some past martial artist found the same technique, which became lost through time.

It is this concept of uncovering old techniques and continuously developing them that is at the core of my Latigo y Daga training method. The techniques presented here are the result of 45 years of whip training by me, 18 of which represent my research into the techniques of the Filipino martial arts, and the ongoing process of uncovery.

The Latigo y Daga method has two distinct principles: (1) it is not designed to directly teach the whip, but rather to teach body mechanics most suited to proper whip manipulation, and (2) since the goal is the development of a particular type of body mechanics, the foundation and corresponding technical progression become critical. The Latigo y Daga training structure consists of specific training blocks that develop a particular group of body mechanics. In turn, this group of body mechanics becomes the foundation for the next block of training and techniques.

Completion of all the training blocks of the Latigo y Daga method provides the martial arts student with a sound foundation in body mechanics, as found in the Filipino arts, and the ability to apply these movements to combative applications of the whip.

The purpose of this text is to document modern Filipino whip techniques in order to preserve them for future generations of martial artists. This will ensure that all practitioners of the whip arts will have a sound technical foundation to continue their own study of the flexible weapons of the Filipino martial arts.

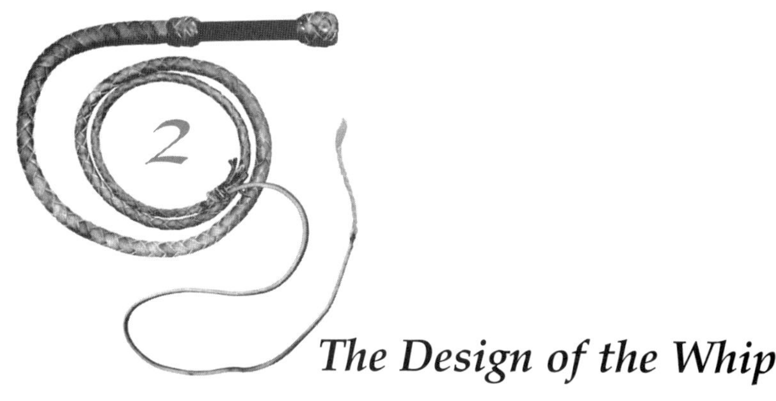

The Design of the Whip

The whip was the first device invented by man that was capable of breaking the sound barrier. The design of the whip doesn't need to be terribly sophisticated to accomplish this. It can be as simple as a wet towel or a section of rope with a piece of string tied to the end. However, the less sophisticated the design, the greater the effort required to crack and manipulate the whip.

To solve these problems, whip designers have integrated influences from several different areas. Major influences that have governed whip design are sailing, agriculture, animal husbandry, and the laws of physics. The fields of sailing, agriculture, and animal husbandry all share the common element of weaving and braiding techniques.

Sailors, in their pursuit of larger sails to power bigger boats, required ropes that were longer, stronger, and lighter. Generations of such rope makers as Momoy Canete and those before him worked to develop sophisticated braiding techniques to meet these needs. The end product of their research is so voluminous that entire texts and manuals have been devoted solely to nautical braiding and rope tying.

As the agriculturists began to produce large amounts of grain, they needed to sift, separate, and carry it from place to place. Using readily available materials, such as rushes and reeds, the grain producers began to develop rudimentary basket-weaving techniques to create vessels to meet these needs.

As with many of man's endeavors, the pursuit of art entered into basket weaving, and we see the results of this in the detailed pattern work of woven baskets. The African and South American cultures excelled at these arts, and it is not uncommon to find 100-year-old baskets woven so tightly that they are still capable of holding water. This type of tight weaving and complex patterns was adapted by whip makers for their whips and is still in use today.

Animal husbandry required harnesses for the draft animals, saddles for the horses, and strongly woven ropes for various tasks. Herding large groups of animals provided the herdsman with hours of idle time, much of which was used to develop complex braiding patterns for harnesses and related equipment. In time, harness and saddle making became a separate trade of its own. This tradition still thrives today and is found at the highest level in the Australian, New Zealand, and Western American leatherworkers. The finely woven, perfectly tapered whips that we use today are the end product of integrating all the skills found in these various trades and disciplines.

WHY THE WHIP CRACKS

To fully understand whip construction and evolution, you must first explore the laws of physics that govern why the whip cracks. The principal law that explains why a whip functions as it does is the law of conservation of energy: energy can neither be mechanically created nor destroyed. The thong of the whip (the braided portion extending from the end of the grip to the woven knot where the thong attaches to the fall) does not create energy; it simply transfers the energy of the user's body to the tip of the whip. The energy begins in the handle, travels down the thong of the whip, and is then converted into heat and sound. The heat comes from the combined friction of the whip moving through the air and the individual braids of the whip stretching and rubbing together. The sound comes from the tip of the whip breaking the sound barrier. The resulting combined energy of heat and sound that is created equals the energy the user puts into the handle of the whip.

The law of conservation of energy is classically described as the product of the velocity of the whip times the mass of the whip. This is how this law is normally shown: $m_1v_1 = m_2v_2$ (the mass of object 1 times the velocity of object 1 equals the mass of object 2 times the velocity of object 2). In this case, the m_1v_1 refers to the butt of the whip and the m_2v_2 refers to the tip of the whip. This means that if you multiply the velocity of the whip by its mass, you will always get the same number whether you measure the velocity and mass at the heavy butt of the whip or at the lighter tip of the popper.

What this means from the whip's standpoint is that as the velocity travels from the whip's handle down the taper of the whip, the same velocity is applied to a constantly decreasing amount of mass. Since the quantity of energy must always be balanced on both sides of the equation, the whip must pick up speed to maintain this balance. Thus, the whip tends to accelerate as it travels through its arc of motion until the very tip of the popper reaches approximately 750 miles per hour, which is the average speed of sound at sea level. At this point, the characteristic crack is heard.

The best practical means of expressing the related laws of physics is created by a device that tapers as smoothly as is physically possible from one end to the other. A small knot near the end, or an uneven taper, will not prevent a whip from cracking but will greatly increase the amount of effort required to generate the cracking sound. This has forced whip makers to continually develop braiding and manufacturing methods that allow them to more closely approximate the theoretical perfect taper. This need for a perfect taper explains why, despite having thousands of years of development, the external appearance of the whip has changed little.

Scientific Documentation of Breaking the Sound Barrier

There has been much controversy over the years as to what actually makes the cracking sound of the whip. Fortunately, physicists thoroughly researched and documented the "physics of whip cracking" in a 1958 study published in the *Journal of the Acoustical Society of America*. This analysis used high-speed photography to study the shock wave created by the tip of the whip. This study documented that as the tip of the whip reaches the speed of sound, the pressure wave behind the popper reverses direction and becomes a forward pressure wave. This study proved that the tip of the whip breaks the sound barrier and produces a miniature sonic boom.

For the serious whip user, this study is important because it explains why the whip will sometimes emit a very small crack and at other times a very loud crack. The amount of air displaced by the popper is proportional to the volume of the sonic boom created. Thus, when you get a little "baby crack" it is because the overall energy is lower and you are only moving a small portion of the popper through the sound barrier. With an extremely well-made whip and good body mechanics, it is possible to move a significantly greater portion of the popper through the sound barrier, which creates a much larger sonic boom.

PARTS OF THE WHIP

From a design standpoint, whips can be broken down into two general types: those with handles and those without handles. Both types have similar components: grip, upper and lower knobs, thong, fall, and popper.

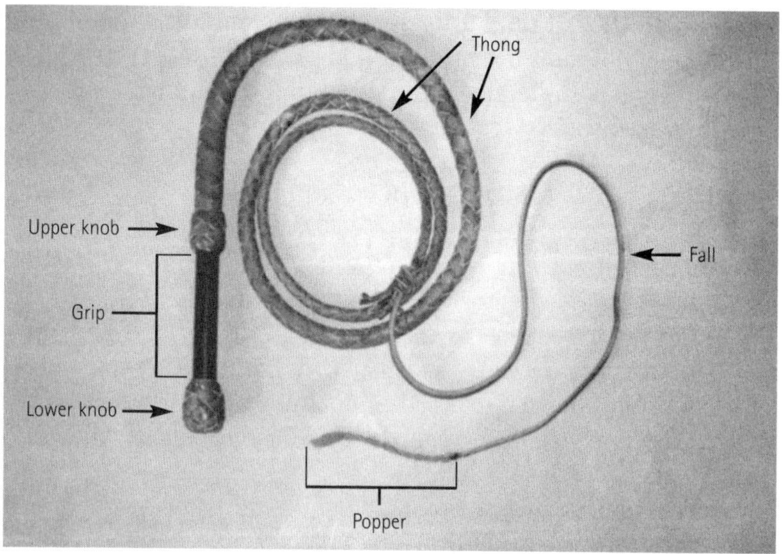

A standard Western bullwhip with the individual parts identified.

The *grip* of the whip varies in length from 4 inches up to a foot. Some whips have both an upper and lower knob, whereas others have only the lower knob. As explained earlier, the *thong* of the whip is the braided portion extending from the end of the grip to the woven knot where the thong attaches to the fall. The *fall* is a thin piece of leather that absorbs most of the punishment generated by the end of the whip. The *popper* is very short, usually about 6 inches long, and comes in a variety of designs. Both the popper and the fall are considered expendable portions of the whip and are easily replaced.

Many of the whip parts are not visible from the outside. For example, the *internal handle* is a metal or fiberglass rod that the whip is woven around. The length of this handle has a strong influence on whip function. It is important not to confuse this handle with the external grip, since the internal handle is often longer than the external grip. Snake whips omit this rod entirely and yet still retain the outer grip. In the case of the Australian stock whip, a completely external handle is used, with the grip woven around the lower portion of the handle.

WHIP CONSTRUCTION

Choosing the proper hide is the first step in making a whip. Kangaroo hide has been the choice of top-quality whip makers for many years because of its superior flexibility and strength. Kangaroos are as common in Australia as rodents are in the rest of the world and are perceived as a similar type of nuisance, so their hides are readily available. But despite this availability, some makers prefer cowhide.

Each hide has its own characteristics, and the experienced whip maker will evaluate each hide's flexibility, density, and grain pattern. These properties ultimately govern the characteristics of the whips woven from each hide.

Once he has chosen the hide, the whip maker carefully cuts long, tapered strips to begin the braiding. He tapers the strips along their length and bevels them on their edges. This process must be done by hand, and the skills required are what separate the great whip makers from the rest.

A high-quality whip is, in fact, two or more whips braided on top of each other. The first internal whip is called the *core*, or *belly*, of the whip. Most whip makers consider the belly of the whip to be one of the most important elements of its construction. Cheaper whips use a rope belly, whereas high-quality ones have a braided belly or use leather strips with a cover sewn over them.

Correct beveling and tapering, combined with proper tensioning during the braiding process, allow each of the internal core pieces to fit tightly together. The other internal whips are then braided over this core. The last whip, the outer portion, has the finest and tightest braiding.

The individual strands that form the whip are woven into a single braid called a *plait,* and a top-quality whip can use anywhere from 12 to 24 strands. The number of strands greatly affects the weight and balance of the whip and, to some degree, the durability. Although allowing a greater range of braiding patterns and colors, 24-plaited whips suffer somewhat in durability because the braids are thinner and smaller.

Attached to the end of the braided portion is the fall. Like the braided thong, the fall greatly influences the functioning of the whip. The fall has to curve and bend more tightly than the rest of the whip and is subject to physical impact from the ground and other objects, so it tends to wear out more quickly. Because of this, it is designed to be changed easily, which allows different falls to be used to fine-tune each whip for a specific purpose, whether it is target work, sport cracking, or animal herding.

Attached to the fall is the popper, the portion that actually breaks the sound barrier. The popper is also expendable; attached to the fall with a simple knot, it can be changed in seconds. As with the fall, the popper can be used to fine-tune the whip. The range of poppers available is limited only by the user's imagination.

In a top-quality whip, the type of fall and popper used largely determines its performance. The subtlest tuning of the whip is done with the choice of the popper. An inexpensive or poorly made whip can be totally insensitive to the popper used. A finely made whip, because of its being nearer the perfect theoretical taper, can be highly sensitive to the popper used, since the popper is the completion of the taper.

Whip makers have their own set of poppers they sell for use with their whips, and they are continually experimenting with new designs. Poppers can be designed to cut paper, crack loudly or softly, or hold up under rough conditions. The choice of the correct popper is the ultimate means of fine-tuning a whip's action.

The whip that results from integrating all of these individual components reflects each maker's criteria for the perfect whip.

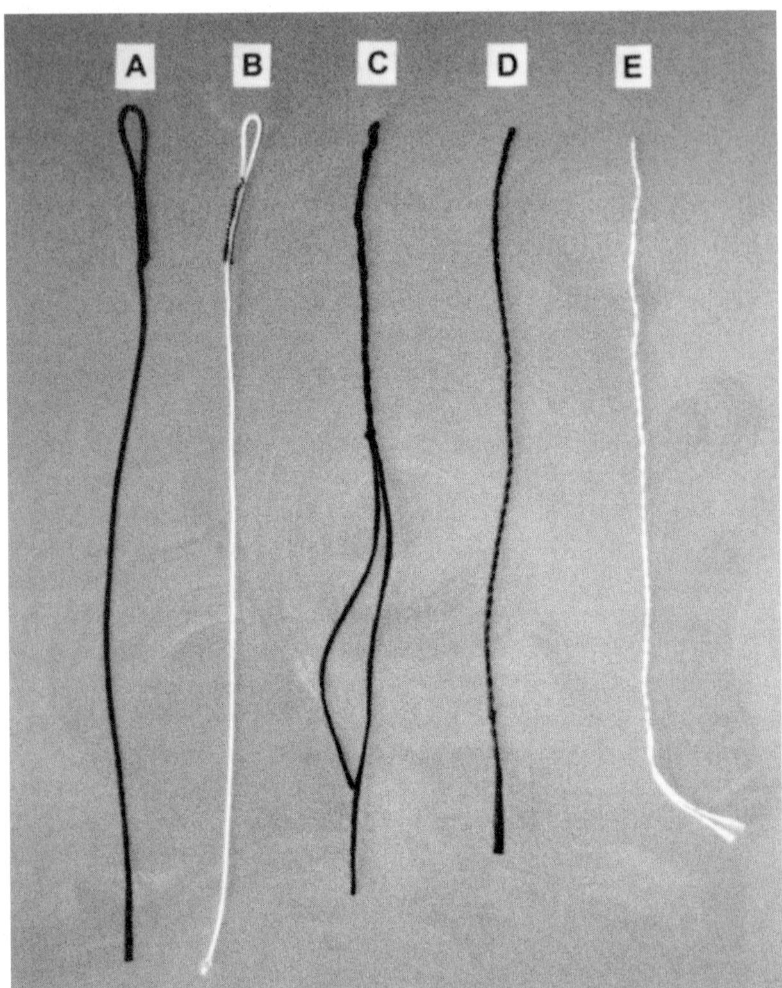

A selection of poppers offered by New Zealand whip maker Peter Jack. The differences in length, diameter, and twist affect how each popper cracks. The following are Peter Jack's descriptions for the function of each of these poppers: (A) great for target work with a very sharp crack, (B) less accurate but long-lasting, general-purpose cracker, (C) snake tongue—half-twisted to give phase pitch effect when cracked at different power levels, (D) twisted poly-waxed bow string, (E) Australian-style, twisted-type, static-discharge cracker for low-level subsonic pops.

Each maker has his own particular goals in terms of weight, overall balance, and ease of manipulation. Such modern whip makers as Joe Strain, Peter Jack, and the venerable David Morgan have pursued the highest level of whip design and construction, resulting in whips that crack so effortlessly they almost seem to do it themselves. This is no accident; these men understand the physics involved and have worked for many years to develop the necessary level of construction skills. The whips made by these men and their contemporaries can be so distinctive that an experienced user, with his eyes closed, can tell the maker of a whip just from the feel alone.

TYPES OF WHIPS

To catalog all the types of whips available in the world today would require an encyclopedia all its own. With this in mind, this overview will focus on the most common types of whips and their applications.

The majority of whips found in general use today are working whips specifically designed to control animals. Working whips can be broken down into two categories, flexible and rigid. In the flexible-whip category are bullwhips, stock whips, the DeLongis whip, snake whips, and custom whips. The rigid-whip category includes coach whips and riding crops. Less common are the nonworking whips, which include fighting whips and improvised whips.

Flexible Whips

Bullwhip

The bullwhip is found predominately in the American West and to some degree in Australia. It is characterized by a grip approximately 8 inches in length, an internal handle about 12 inches long, and an overall length of 4 to 16 feet. A bullwhip longer than 16 feet is difficult to manipulate in the field and is considered a "trick" whip rather than a working tool.

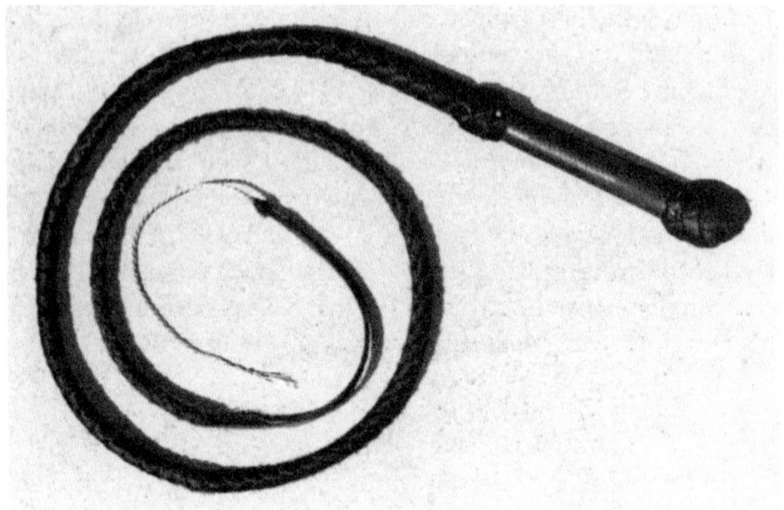

An economy nylon whip made by Colorado Saddlery.

Some bullwhips have swiveling handles, which are supposed to make it easier for the novice to use. At the most basic skill level, the swivel handle may do this, but ultimately it greatly limits what the whip can do, particularly in the area of accuracy.

An American innovation is the nylon bullwhip braided entirely from half-inch-wide nylon strips. Such whips have proven to be durable, impervious to wet weather, and responsive. These factors, combined with a price in the $70 range, have made them very popular. They are both economical and durable, but ultimately they limit the skill development of the user. This limitation is due principally to the technical reality that half-inch-wide nylon strips cannot be braided to the small-diameter taper found in high-quality leather whips. The fact that the strips cannot be tapered as narrowly at the tip means that the whip requires a greater input of energy to crack and thus is less sensitive to small movements of the user.

Another type of nylon bullwhip, known as a Florida stock whip or cow whip, is manufactured to a much higher standard. This type is typically made with 12 to 24 plaits of nylon parachute cord. Unlike leather whips, these nylon whips are unaffected by moisture and are designed to work well in a wet or humid environment. They are very similar in design to an Australian stock whip and use a 16-inch handle, with a thong of 4 to 8 feet in length. The Florida stock whip, in a 6-foot length, is the style used by practitioners of the Sayoc kali whip system, which has integrated the dagger with this whip to form the core of its whip training program.

Some makers are now using this type of nylon cord to make snake whips and bullwhips, and these whips are gaining in popularity because of their reasonable cost and moisture resistance.

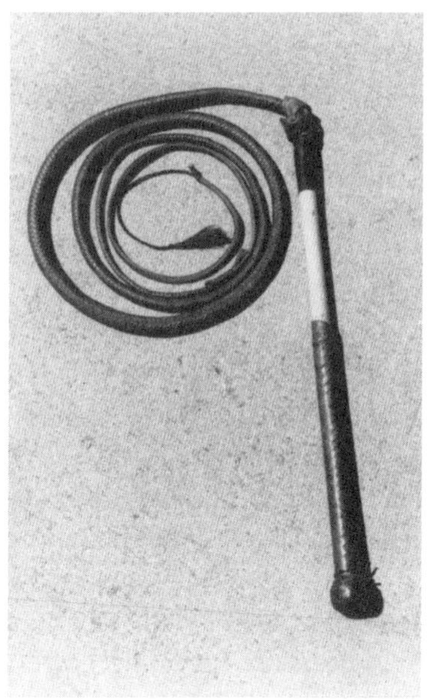

An Australian stock whip of traditional design, with a portion of the cane handle exposed.

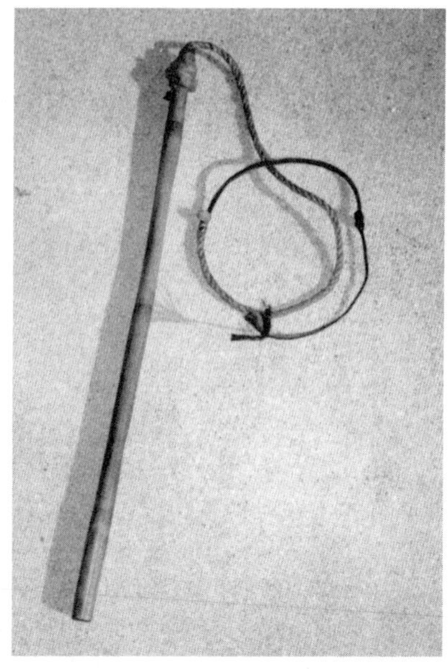

A Filipino stock whip as used in the Doce Pares system.

Stock Whip

Stock whips are predominantly of Australian or New Zealand design. They have handles that run from 14 to 28 inches in length, with 18 inches being about the average. The handle is generally made of a type of cane found in Australia and New Zealand. This cane is similar to rattan in flexibility and strength and is ideal for whip handles.

The handle is usually braided over at its upper and lower ends, with the cane exposed in the middle. In some cases, the entire cane handle is wrapped in leather. Whip makers who do this often treat this portion of the whip as their artistic palette and weave very intricate patterns in this area.

The knot that joins the handle to the thong is called the *keeper knot,* which is unique to whip makers in Australia and New Zealand, and the degree of flexibility it provides allows rapid directional changes when cracking the whip.

The Filipinos have a unique variant of their own in the stock whip pattern. This whip has a rattan handle of approximately 28 inches, with an equal length of rope attached and a popper tied at the end of the rope. This whip can function as both a rigid goad and a normal stock whip. A farmer or fieldworker using readily available raw materials can easily make this simple type of whip.

DeLongis Whip

Developed by Anthony DeLongis with whip maker Terry Jacka, the DeLongis whip is a special hybrid of the stock whip and the bullwhip. This kangaroo-hide whip is made in the bullwhip pattern, but the standard internal handle is lengthened to match the traditional stock-whip handle. This gives the whip a unique action and exceptional accuracy.

DeLongis developed this whip to increase accuracy when working with a partner in his film work and to slightly increase the distance of the whip from his mount when performing stunts and complex combinations from horseback. This whip is made in 6-, 7-

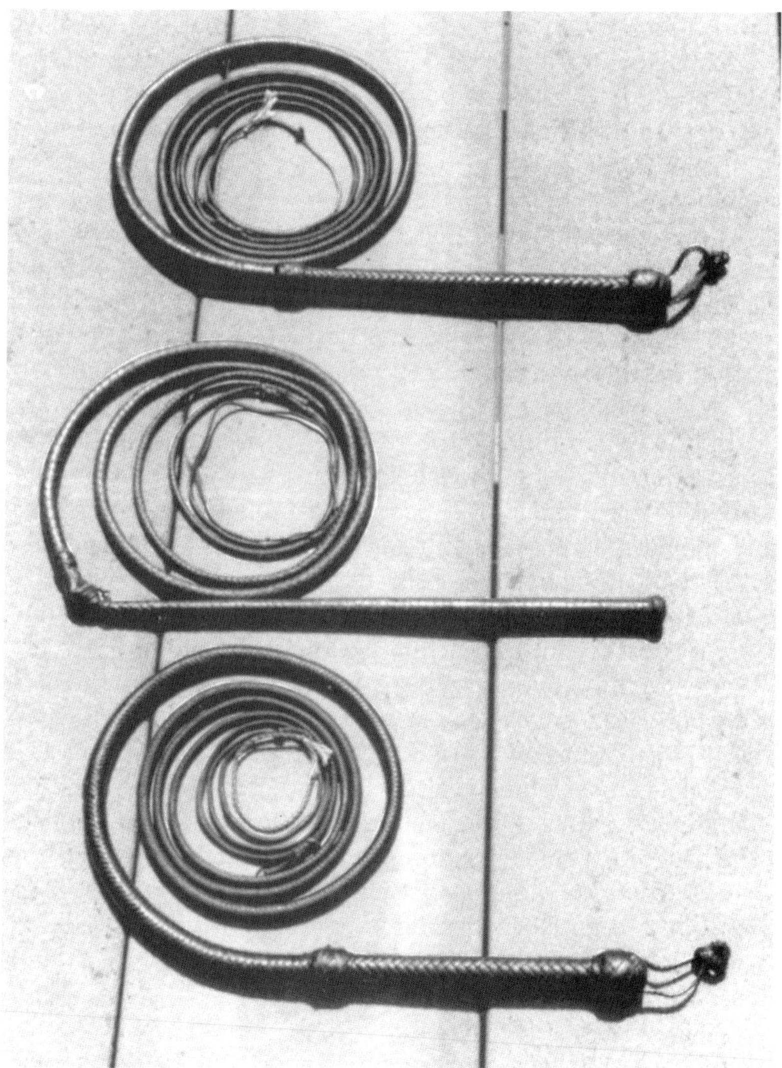

A high-quality whip in the standard Western bullwhip pattern (bottom), an Australian stock whip with the standard-length handle fully braided over (middle), and a DeLongis hybrid whip (top). Note how the length of the DeLongis handle compares with the handle of the other two whips.

, and 8-foot lengths using the traditional Australian method of measuring only the braided body of the whip, and not counting the additional 3 feet of fall and popper. The feel of this whip is unique and opens up a whole new field of manipulation to the user.

Snake Whips

Cowboys out on the range have very limited space for carrying gear and supplies, so they needed a more compact whip. By leaving out the internal handle of the whip, a compact short whip, known as a snake whip, was developed that could be conveniently coiled and carried in saddlebags or jacket pockets.

Snake whips are usually 3 to 5 feet long and come in two varieties. The first is a fully tapered whip with the popper woven directly into the thong. Though it requires significantly more work to replace the popper, this type of whip more closely approaches the optimal theoretical taper than any other type. The second variety uses the more traditional separate thong and fall.

Since snake whips are very short and lack a handle, they tend to be too light to function well. It is common to sew lead shot into a thin, round, cloth bag; insert the bag where the handle would be; and weave the whip around this bag, thus increasing the mass of the whip and greatly improving its action. This practice of shot-loading is also used in bullwhip construction to change the action of the whip. Two other variations of snake whips are the signal whip and dog quirt. Signal whips are shot-loaded whips in 3- and 4-foot lengths designed specifically for sled-dog racers. Dog quirts are very short whips carried as a symbol of authority by dog handlers in field trials.

Custom Whips

Whip customization falls into two categories. The first is tailoring a whip for a specific purpose, such as cutting-type tricks, or for creating a particular balance for sport whip cracking. The second category is incorporating cosmetic or aesthetic changes into the

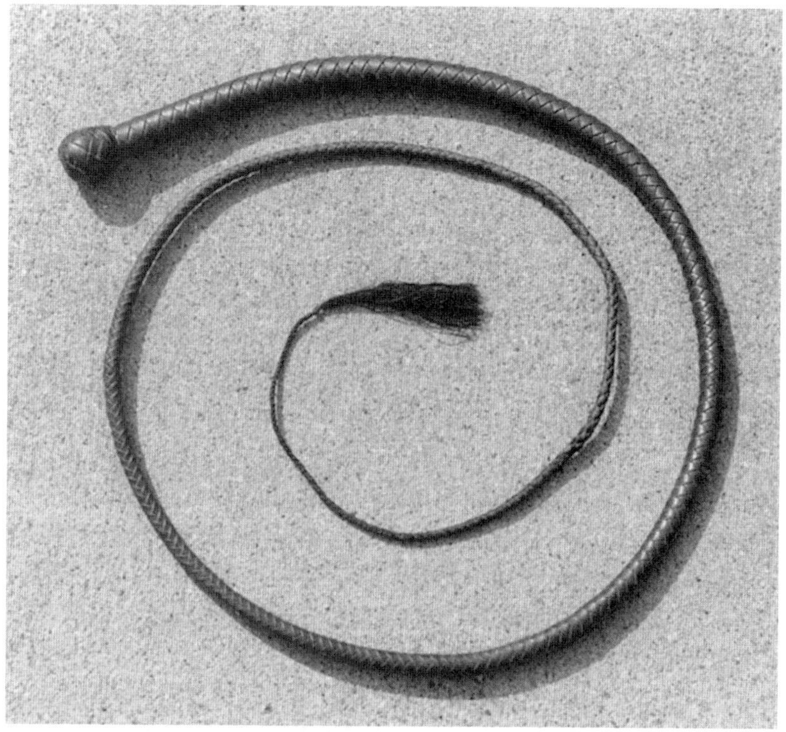

A signal whip by Joe Strain with the cracker braided directly into the end of the whip. This type of whip does not use a fall.

whip, such as adding detail work on the handle or multi-colored braiding patterns. Leather can be dyed virtually any color: red, green, black, brown, and white whips are common. The variety of options in this area is limited only by the purchaser's imagination and the whip maker's tolerance for custom orders.

Australian whip maker Si Davey has taken the natural skin patterns of the venomous snakes of Australia and duplicated them in his braided whips. These are made as 3-foot snake-style whips. The patterns and colors are so accurate that if these whips are positioned in grass, they could easily be mistaken for an actual snake.

Anthony DeLongis owns a pair of custom whips with the handles made out of preserved cobra heads. Unique in the whip world, this pair of whips exemplifies the kind of creativity that can be done in custom work. Roger Patterson made both snakeheads and attached one to a whip of his own spiral-braid design and the other to a traditional latigo whip braided by master whip maker Leonard Wheatley. The Patterson whip is unique in that it has a spiral braiding pattern on the thong and uses a braided fall. This combination gives the whip a very distinctive action not found in other whips.

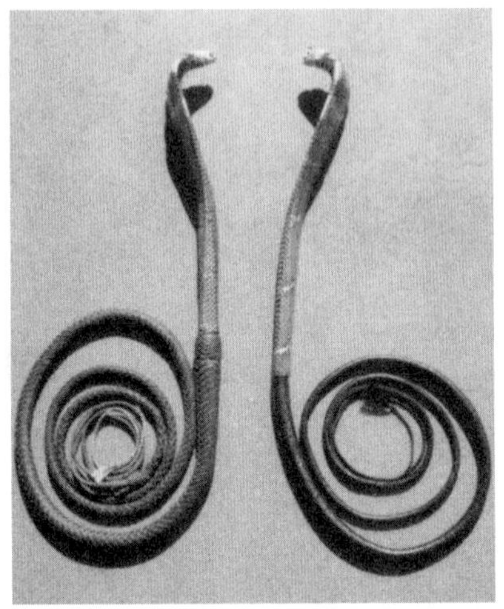

DeLongis' cobra-headed whips: the Leonard Wheatley (left) and Roger Patterson whips.

The cobra head on the Patterson whip.

Rigid Whips

Coach Whips

Coach whips have the longest handle of all the types, with handles often 4 to 6 feet in length and thongs that are typically as long as the handle. The longer han-

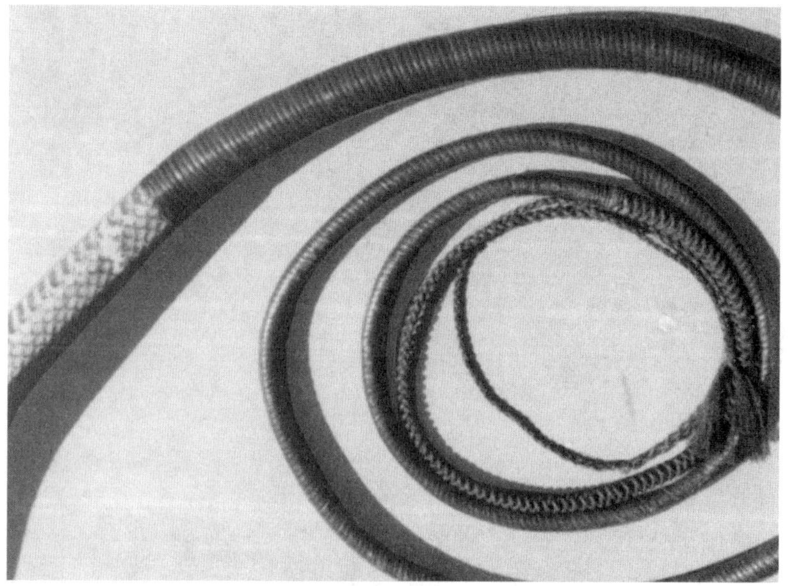

A close-up view of the unique spiral braid used on the Patterson whip.

dles allow the wielder to reach those animals that are farther away without disturbing the ones that are closer. This would be important for drivers of horse-drawn carriages, for example, because they may have to control two or three teams of horses. Coach whips are generally used while the wielder is seated but can be used while he is standing on the ground to train horses in the ring. Modern mass-produced coach whips are usually made of braided nylon, although most whip makers can make leather ones for a custom order.

Riding Crops

Riding crops are very short rigid whips, usually 12 to 24 inches in length, with a small looped flap of leather at the tip. Older-style riding crops were often made with an ornately

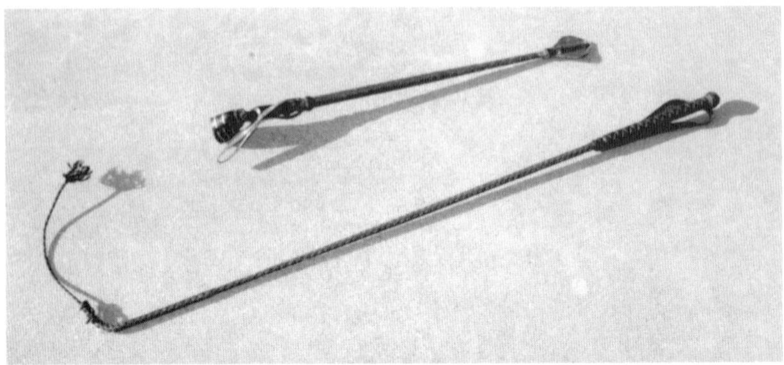

A 3-foot coach whip (foreground) and an African riding crop (background).

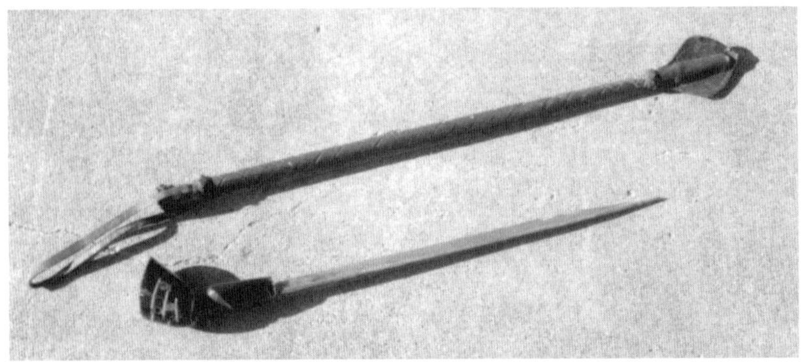

The African riding crop carries a dagger in the handle. The concept of having a riding crop with a dagger in the handle is fairly common throughout the world and is also used in East Indian elephant goads.

woven cover braided over a leather or wooden core. Some of these concealed a knife or spike incorporated into the handle. Contemporary mass-produced riding crops are made with fiberglass cores, woven nylon covers, and molded rubber handles.

Combative Whips

"Then there was William Meharry, herding cattle in Champaign County. He rode horseback, snapping off rattlesnake heads with a long cattle whip, sometimes killing twenty-five in a day."

—Carl Sandburg, *Abraham Lincoln: The Prairie Years* (1926)

At some point, man has taken virtually every tool or implement he has ever used and turned it into a weapon. This was almost always the result of field expediency when animals or other men attacked during the normal course of life. The remarkable efficiency of farm tools used as weapons has resulted in entire fields of the martial arts being devoted to the mastery of various agricultural tools for self-defense. This is clearly seen in the many Chinese systems of kung fu that have techniques for the hoe, monk's spade, ax, and other farm implements. The whip is no exception to this tendency to use farm tools as weapons, and examples of fighting whips are found on all continents. Fighting whips are not to be confused with multiple-tailed whips and other types designed only to inflict pain. Despite having some historical significance, these types of whips are not discussed in this text.

FILIPINO WHIPS

Latiko Horsewhip of Pananandata

The *latiko* is a type of Filipino horsewhip with a heavily knotted tip and lash. The lash portion is knotted over its entire length and is considerably more rigid than the braided lash of more traditional horse whips. The Filipino latiko is one of the traditional flexible weapons of the Pananandata system taught by Grandmaster Amante P. Marinas Sr. Considered a world authority on the latiko, Grandmaster Marinas has been using this whip since his childhood in the Philippines and has written extensively on it.

Grandmaster Marinas believes that the latiko requires no modification to become a fighting whip: "A hit of the latiko is excruciatingly painful. Properly wielded, the latiko is a terrifying weapon. It is aimed mainly at the arm or face."

Grandmaster Marinas demonstrates with his son how the latiko would be used against an attacker using double-latiko techniques.

Grandmaster Marinas demonstrates how the latiko would be used against an empty-hand attacker.

The knotted tip and lash add to the weight of the whip and greatly increase its effectiveness in combat. It is easy to see how the latiko, being readily at hand for the carriage driver, could instantly become an effective weapon against attack, whether from wild animals or individuals.

Rope Bullwhip

Rope whips of any design can be as devastating as a leather whip, but they are generally lighter, which limits the amount of power they can produce. As a rule, a heavier whip generates more power. To compensate, whip makers often add knots to a rope whip over its entire length to make it heavier. This allows the whip to deliver more energy to the target and thus increase its combat effectiveness. The addition of these knots is seen in the latiko whips used by Grandmaster Marinas and also in the rope whips designed, braided, and used by Grandmaster Momoy Canete.

Grandmaster Canete's personal whips were made in the Filipino rope bullwhip pattern, but he also integrated the knotting principle used in the latiko horsewhip. His whips were quite heavy because of the number of knots used. Grandmaster Canete took combat very seriously, and his whip designs clearly reflected their use as combat weapons.

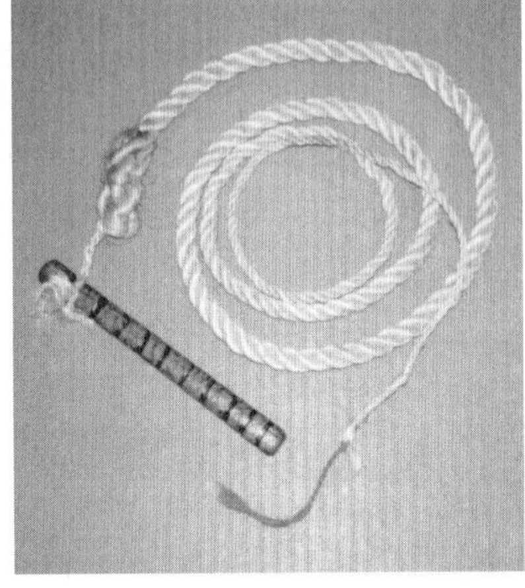

A rope whip identical in design to the one used by Momoy Canete.

Rope Stock Whip

The Filipino stock whip is essentially a rattan baton with a section of manila rope attached to the end. Makers of rope whips in the Filipino stock-whip pattern compensate for the lack of mass in the rope portion of the whip by attaching it to a rattan baton to add mass and strength. This allows the rope-style stock whip to function equally effectively as a stock whip or straight baton. This characteristic is what moves this type of whip into the combative whip category.

By gripping the rope portion of the whip at the base of the handle, any Filipino stylist with basic stick training can take this type of stock whip and effectively use it for all the normal strikes and blocks found in the Filipino arts. With specialized training, he can then use the rope portion of the whip for striking and binding the opponent. When the basic stick skills are integrated with the rope whip skills, the Filipino fighter wielding this whip can effortlessly transition from baton work to whip work at will.

The Filipino stock whip gripped for use as a baton.

The Filipino stock whip held for use as a whip.

Stingray Fishtail

The stingray fishtail is similar in size and appearance to a riding crop. It ranges from 12 to 30 inches in length and requires no modification for combative purposes. Although it can be used effectively as a riding crop, it is mainly used as a weapon and also in spiritual rituals.

As discussed in Chapter 1, the stingray is a bottom-feeding fish whose skin is subject to much abrasion as it scours the ocean floor for food. The stingray has developed what is known as "dermal denticles," referring to the fact that its underbelly skin is actual dental material, which makes it very coarse and abrasion resistant. This skin and to some degree the tail have a texture much like coarse sandpaper. The telson on the end contains a poison. Generally, when the stingray tail is dried after removal, the telson dries out as well and becomes brittle, and will usually break off just from normal handling.

A single strike with the stingray tail will grind through the skin and leave a mark similar to the "road rash" you get when falling off a bicycle onto pavement. Because of its light weight, the stingray fishtail whip has limited striking power, so in the past some wielders would coat the tail with poison. The poison was easily retained in the coarse surface of the whip and transferred directly into the abraded wound.

The primary target for the ray tail is the face because of its soft skin and the tendency for facial wounds to bleed profusely. Just as with the rope stock whip, all the typical baton striking patterns and defenses directly apply to the stingray tail. An experienced Filipino stylist can instantly apply his techniques to the stingray tail.

Caution: Always be cautious when training with or using an authentic stingray tail because of the possible presence of poison, which can easily be transferred to either the wielder or his adversary.

INDONESIAN WHIPS

The range of technical material and weaponry found in the Indonesian martial arts is quite diverse and worthy of a complete study of its own. The whip is included in these arts, and there are several references to them in Donn Draeger's book *Weapons and Fighting Arts of the Indonesian Archipelago.*

Draeger describes several whip arts in Indonesia, including *tjambuk,* a secret whip-fighting technique displayed only during a special folk dance. The whip used in this dance is called a *chemeti,* which is made of buffalo hide, human hair, or metal chain. The chemeti has a handle of hard leather or hardwood wrapped with leather, with an overall length of 3 to 5 feet.

Draeger describes another system called *udung* or *tiban,* which uses a whip called the *petjat.* The petjat is 4 to 6 feet in length and is made of strong, twisted coconut-palm fibers. This whip resembles the *sjambok* (the traditional whip of South Africa; the name seems to have originated as *cambuk* in Indonesia) in appearance. The petjat's use is principally ceremonial; it is believed that the whip's action will produce needed rain. Draeger describes the elder practitioners of these systems as having fantastic skills and arms that are masses of scar tissue from years of training. The scar tissue allows them to take whiplash strikes on their arms without feeling pain.

Noted Indonesian silat instructor Guru Besar/Pendekar Herman Suwanda was highly skilled with the whip, and applications of these skills are evident in the techniques he taught for use with a rolled-up sarong. The rolled sarong has considerable mass concentrated in a small area and can produce a remarkable amount of striking force. Video footage of Pendekar Suwanda shows him striking to the groin with enough power to lift his opponent off the ground. Pendekar Suwanda's sister Guru Besar Rita Suwanda has preserved and now teaches the family system of Pencak Silat Mande Muda.

AFRICAN SJAMBOK

"A blow from one of these will open a man up like a straight razor."

—Peter Capstick

The sjambok is a unique rigid whip that resembles an animal goad more than a true whip, with characteristics of both. Highly functional as a goad, it also has the most devastating ability to inflict pain. The sjambok is so effective at inflicting pain that it is standard police issue for riot control in South Africa.

A typical sjambok of traditional manufacture is 3 to 6 feet in length and tapers from 1 inch at the base to 1/2 inch at the tip. Strips of rhinoceros or hippopotamus hide are cut to a taper and then rolled between heavy plates of steel until the desired shape is achieved. Modern sjamboks are made of synthetic plastic or rubber. They are approximately 5/8 inch at the butt and taper to 3/8 inch at the tip. Currently, they are mass produced, quite serviceable, and inexpensive as well.

The sjambok has a broad range of fighting techniques specific to its design. In fact, the range is so great that James Loriega has written an entire book on the subject, *The Scourge of the Dark Continent: The Martial Use of the African Sjambok,* which is recommended reading for anyone interested in combative applications of the whip.

Lynn Thompson, the founder and president of Cold Steel products, sells modern sjamboks made of densely compressed rubber. These are identical to those issued to the South African

Professor Ron Lew demonstrates how to properly grip a police-issue sjambok, with the loop at the end secured around the wrist.

riot police. In *The Scourge of the Dark Continent,* Loriega quotes Thompson on the combative power of the sjambok: "A light blow can raise a serious welt, while a heavy stroke can cut through thick clothing like rotten cheesecloth, leaving a fearsome wound, and is guaranteed to deter virtually any aggressor."

The African sjambok is similar to the Filipino stingray tail in both physical construction and technical application. Both are flexible whips made from coarse animal hide, come in a variety of similar lengths, and inflict comparable types of damage. These similarities provide considerable crossover between Filipino stingray tail techniques and the ones Loriega describes for the sjambok. Like other rigid whips, the sjambok is totally compatible with Filipino stick techniques, and the shorter sjamboks can be wielded in the same fashion as the stingray tail.

STEEL WHIPS

Steel is a highly unusual material for whip construction because it it is much harder to work with than leather, and steel whips are difficult to design so that they actually crack. Clearly any steel whip is designed specifically for combat or as an exercise in craftsmanship. Three types of steel whips are the ribbon band whips from India, the medieval chain mail whip, and the Chinese chain whip.

Ribbon Band Whips from India

The area formerly referred to as East India has developed an astonishing array of combative weapons, including the whip family. Inhabitants of this area have created a unique fighting whip that resembles a sword, but which has two or four long steel bands instead of a rigid blade. With sharply pointed ends on the bands, this whip is admirably suited to warfare and, when used with a shield, brings new meaning to the term *mayhem* on the battlefield.

Chain Mail Whips

The manufacture of medieval chain mail is a 1,500-year-old art. Excellent examples of chain mail armor can be seen in museums throughout the world. It is not known whether chain mail whips were actually used during medieval times, but considering the enormous range of weapons developed then and the suitability of chain link to whip making, it is very likely that they were. Its resistance to being cut with a blade and its ability to effectively reach around a shield would have made this type of whip invaluable on the medieval battlefield.

Over the past 30 years, medieval re-creation groups have generated a strong demand for medieval-type weapons, resulting in a new generation of artisans skilled in weapons manufacture. One such artisan, Michael DeVeny, is a master-level craftsman who makes chain mail whips in 40-, 60-, and 80-inch lengths. He hand-makes each whip from stainless-steel links and guarantees them for life. He refers to his 80-inch whip as

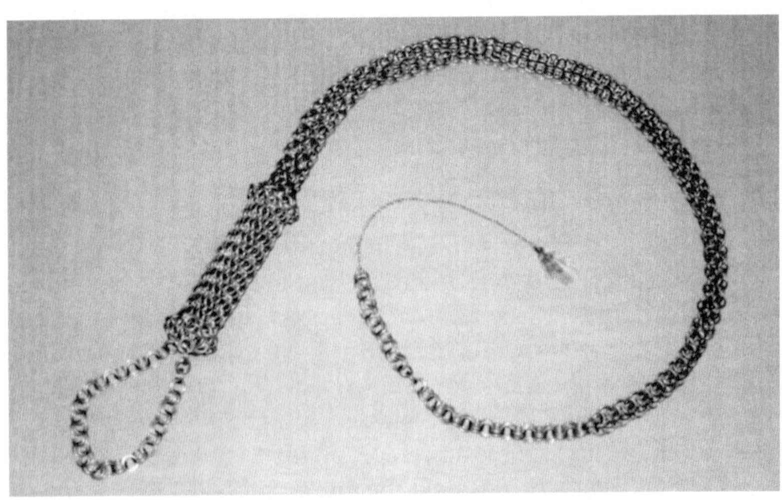

A Michael DeVeny chain mail whip coiled like a typical leather whip.

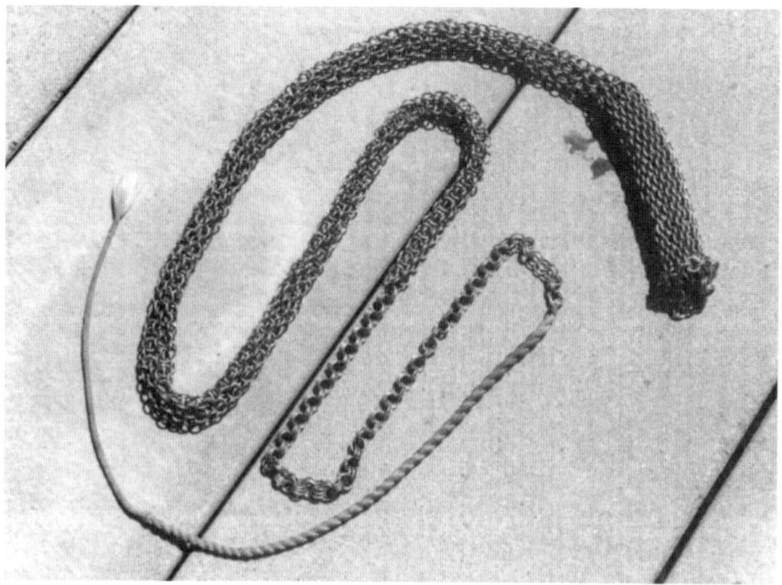

The chain mail whip coiled to show its true flexibility.

"The Beast" due to the difficulty in keeping it under proper control. The chain mail whip requires a completely different set of manipulation techniques from that required for a normal whip. The chain mail whip has to be under continuous outward tension during its use. If that tension dissipates, it will literally lose all its shape and collapse into what appears to be a large handful of small, joined steel rings. The wielder must be very skilled to maintain the correct tension; the whip is unforgiving of weak or poor technique and can return and strike the wielder with enormous force.

Anthony DeLongis, a professional whip trainer who trains with chain mail whips, recommends working the whip like a flexible stick to maintain this critical tension. Strikes can be delivered from all angles and should continue through the target before flowing smoothly to the next attack angle. The whip should never be snatched backward, or it will expend its formidable energy into the user's face or body. It is definitely not a whip to be toyed with. The chain mail whip can be coiled like a normal whip or in a zigzag pattern because of its superior flexibility. This flexibility also allows it to fit into a pocket or small saddlebag.

CHINESE CHAIN WHIP

The Chinese martial arts have a seemingly endless array of weapons to study and train with. The Chinese steel whip fits into the flexible-weapons category and traditionally has seven or nine short iron sections joined together with chain rings. The first section is slightly longer than the others and serves as a handle. The business end is a sharp, pointed weight, and

A nine-section Chinese chain whip with a small colored flag at the end to aid visibility during demonstrations.

a flag is usually attached here to distract an opponent or help track the whip during demonstrations. Combatively, it has the ability to wrap around the arms, legs, torso, or neck, and can be used to pull a mounted man off his horse. It has good power as a striking weapon because of its weight and can be used for disarming as well. The chain whip is difficult to master because of the potential for personal injury early on, but once learned, its power and grace make it a very potent weapon for demonstrations.

WESTERN WHIPS

Leather Bullwhip

Any leather whip, regardless of its length, is a formidable fighting weapon. Whereas the shorter whips provide better close-range techniques, a 6- or 8-foot whip is something to be greatly feared in the hands of a skilled user. The leather whip has the ability to cut flesh effortlessly and can break smaller bones in the body through impact alone. It can also be used to wrap and dislocate finger, wrist, and elbow joints. The crack of a heavy leather whip near the head is so powerful that it can cause permanent hearing loss, and any strike to the face is instantly incapacitating. A strike to the throat has enough power to crush the windpipe, ultimately resulting in death. *Caution: Anyone contemplating a study of combative whip training should bear these facts in mind because the leather whip will inflict these types of injuries on the wielder as freely as on an attacker.*

Latigo y Daga Fighting Whip

Any whip can be an effective combat tool. However, just as with any other tool, the best ones have been designed to do a specific job. The Latigo y Daga fighting whip is the end result of three years of my design and research to create a whip specifically for combative applications. Any attempt to deal with all the possible scenarios that can arise in combat rapidly degenerates into theoretic ramblings. To design a combative whip requires some basic assumptions about what the whip will be used for and in what situations, with a focus on the practical rather than the theoretical.

In the case of the Latigo y Daga whip, my primary assumption was that its effective combative range needed to cover everything from grappling range to 10 feet away from the body. The whip is one of very few weapons that can be tailored to do this effectively. I based this range on my experiences with full-contact weapons fighting in the various Filipino tournament groups and, at a much more serious level, the Dog Brothers organization. Marc Denny and Eric Knaus founded Dog Brothers in 1988, and its fights are full contact with sticks, clubs, the bokken, the staff, and virtually any other weapon that is offered, including the whip. Since grappling is allowed, this type of fighting permits real-time experience in the combative range control needed to be successful in this type of fighting.

My second assumption when I designed the Latigo y Daga was that the whip would be used in conjunction with a knife. Using the knife with the whip provides more options for self-protection at close range. Eric has effectively demonstrated that a highly skilled martial artist can evade both long and short whips and then close to grappling range. Though the whip is an admirable close-range grappling tool, the knife adds a much greater margin of security. A flexible whip with a total length of 6 1/2 feet from the popper tip to butt knob provides an effective reach of 10 feet from the user's body. It is also short enough to be twirled rapidly without striking the ground. This whip must be balanced and proportioned so that it will not wrap around or foul the user's own body during use. The need to use the free hand to control or grab the thong of the whip strongly affects the requisite balance and proportion. Lastly, the fall must be strong enough to not break during grappling applications, and it must be able to securely lock on itself when it is used for wrapping.

Through the process of trimming, cutting, rebraiding, and undergoing much trial and error, a whip emerged that met all these criteria. I used a Colorado Saddlery 6-foot cowhide bullwhip as the foundation for the modifications primarily because it is inexpensive (about $60) in case the modifications were unsuccessful. In the final version, I shortened the thong from 64 to 44 inches, reduced the internal handle from 12 to 11 inches, and cut down the grip from 6 to 4 inches. The plaits of the last foot of the thong were retapered, rebeveled, and then tightly braided. A 24-inch kangaroo fall of medium weight and a thin braided-nylon popper completed the whip.

Students who have practiced with this whip quickly learn that it has formidable combative ability. Unfortunately, its excellent bal-

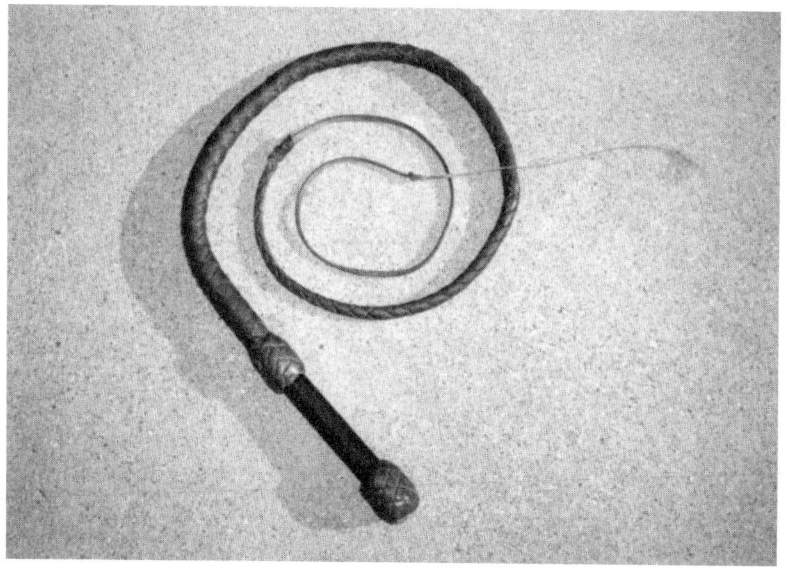

The final version of the Latigo y Daga combat whip, nicknamed the "Frankenwhip."

ance and speed tend to inspire overconfidence, and it can be easily—and very painfully—misjudged. The tendency of this whip to turn on its owner has earned it the nickname of "Frankenwhip."

My search for the "perfect whip" is a classic example of uncovery in action. As it turned out, I discovered that Joe Strain and Peter Jack already produced whips of near identical proportions to the Latigo y Daga whip.

Joe Strain has developed an excellent 4-foot bullwhip in what he calls his Lone Star pattern. The Lone Star is identical in overall dimension to the Latigo y Daga whip but is lighter. The light weight gives the Lone Star a slightly different balance, but this is more than compensated for by its total lack of vices and effortless cracking. The majority of techniques presented in this text were developed using the Lone Star, and I highly recommend this model to any student interested in exploring short-whip techniques.

Peter Jack also designs a whip with the same proportions as the Latigo y Daga fighting whip. Peter's whip is sold specifically as

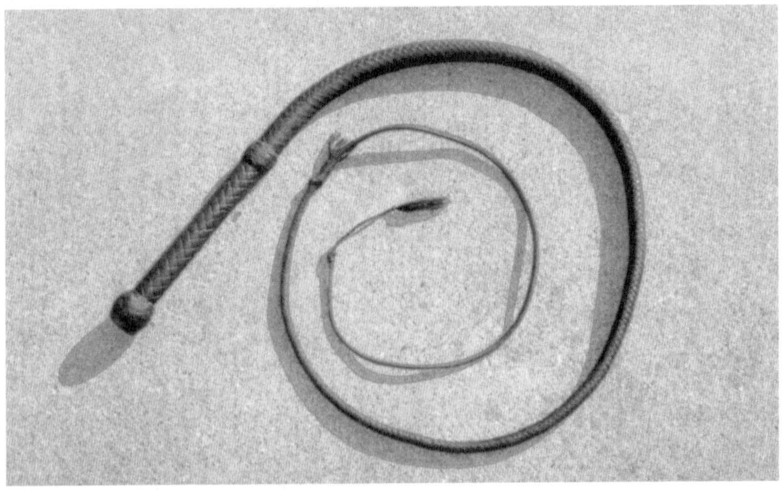

One of the author's personal favorites, a 4-foot Joe Strain Lone Star whip.

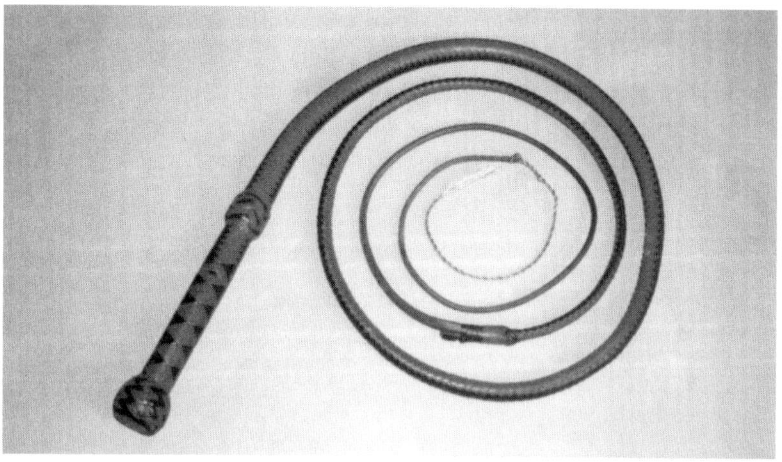

The Peter Jack Self-Defense whip with a custom braiding pattern.

a serious, no-nonsense self-defense whip that permits effortless manipulation. It features a slightly larger butt knob and shot loading. The larger butt knob enables powerful butt strikes, and the extra mass from the shot loading significantly increases the power delivered into the body of an opponent. A strike to the body with any portion of the thong has a significant impact, and when the whip is folded in half and gripped as a flail, it has the same lethal potential as a lead-loaded sap. Using his basic self-defense whip as a foundation, Peter Jack has developed a whip specifically tailored to meet the needs of the students of the Latigo y Daga method, and it is available through him by special order.

Joe Strain's Lone Star whip and the Peter Jack Latigo y Daga whip are both perfectly balanced, finely crafted of the best kangaroo hide, and highly recommended for practicing the techniques presented in this text.

It is clear from this examination of fighting whips that no modification to any type of whip is really necessary to make it an effective combat weapon. Certainly, a whip can be tailored for specific techniques, such as the Latigo y Daga whip, but the basic components of the grip, thong, fall, and popper remain the same. Ultimately it is the quality of the fighting techniques used that determines a whip's combat effectiveness.

Part Two

Training Methods

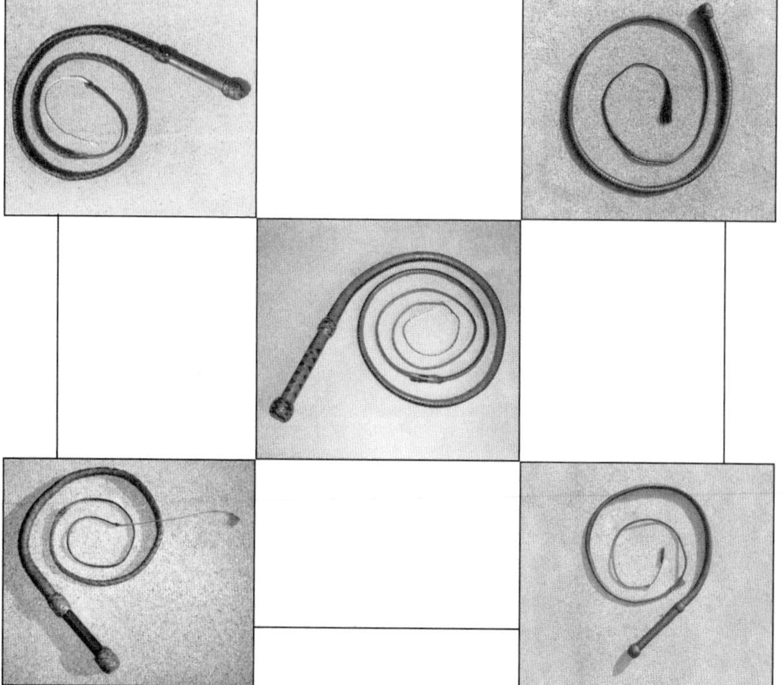

Safety in Whip Training

The purpose of self-defense training is first to protect oneself and, as these abilities develop, to extend that protection to others around you. Many martial artists receive greater injuries in training than they would if they were assaulted. Their logic for training like this is that it is better to take the risks of getting hit in the controlled environment of the training hall than to find out their skills don't work in an actual confrontation.

This logic may hold some validity for general martial arts training, but it does not apply to the whip. *A single mistake in training with the whip can destroy an eye or cause permanent hearing loss.*

Whip training goes through progressive stages. As your confidence builds, you tend to lose some degree of respect for the whip. The old saying "Familiarity breeds contempt" applies quite well in this case. It is easy to become familiar and comfortable with the tip of the whip as it travels at 1,100 feet per second, but that familiarity must never cause one to lose respect for the power a whip can generate.

The handle of the whip moves at slow speeds, and as it transfers its energy down the length of the whip, it builds up tremendous acceleration and speed at the tip of the popper. The popper can travel at 1,100 feet per second, and at that speed it is totally invisible to both the naked eye and conventional video and film. The tip is traveling at a speed that you cannot see, much less pretend that you can react to. The only warning you will ever get that your whip is going to hit you is the pain you feel after it happens.

Caution: There is absolutely no excuse for not wearing eye and ear protection when training with the whip.

Whip practitioners with 20 or 30 years of experience often demonstrate their techniques without safety equipment, but they only demonstrate techniques over which they have perfected their control. They feel safe—and, in fact, they are safe—with those techniques. When practicing or developing new tech-

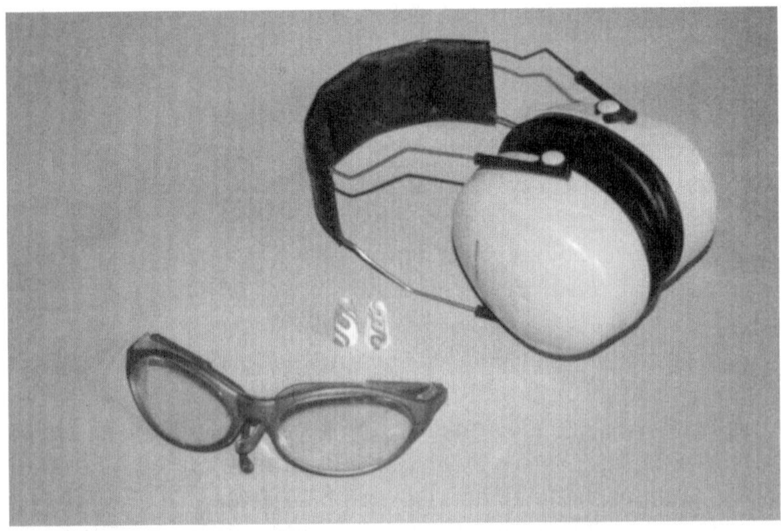

Always wear suitable eye and ear protection when training with the whip.

niques during their personal training, they wear protective gear. An experienced whip stylist has more than likely struck himself hundreds of times with his whip and learned the value of protective gear from those experiences.

One acquaintance, who had used a whip for several years and regularly demonstrated it at martial arts seminars, casually pulled the whip back at one demonstration and struck himself in the eye. He was blind in that eye for three days, but fortunately he later regained normal function in it. He usually wore prescription glasses and had become used to not having to think about safety glasses in his whip training. The day he struck himself in the eye, he happened to be wearing his contact lenses. Examples like this only reinforce the need for safety gear at all times.

There are several schools of thought on safety for whip training. One approach advises wearing safety glasses, a motorcycle helmet, and leather jacket and chaps. Once you are suited up, you are supposed to go out and flog away to your heart's content without fear of injury. You also don't have to worry about developing good technique since this approach presumes that the whip is out of your control. This attitude is fundamentally unsound.

The whip is very much like a gun. It goes exactly where you point it. Just as handgunners spend many hours developing precise aim and control over their weapon, so should the whip practitioner. The whip should receive the same respect as a gun and should be approached at the beginning with the same level of caution. Slow, progressive training is the key to proper whip safety.

Whip users in movie and television productions have to practice absolute safety on the set for their own safety and that of others around them. And they have to do this while creating the illusion of actually hitting or injuring their targets in the film.

Anthony DeLongis is a professional actor, choreographer, stuntman, martial artist, and whip trainer who has developed a complete method of training that provides a complete zone of safety for himself and others on the set. He has trained many Hollywood actors in safe whip techniques, including Michelle Pfeiffer for her part as Catwoman in the *Batman Returns* movie. Any text on whip manipulation would be incomplete without a recommendation to study DeLongis' methods and approach, particularly in the area of safe whip handling.

Western whip artists and Hollywood stuntmen are at complete odds in one respect with the combative whip stylist. The combative stylist is actively training to make contact with the person in front of him. To the Western artist or Hollywood stuntman, this is the worst possible scenario and demonstrates a complete lack of control. Oddly enough, this becomes the common meeting ground for the combative stylist and other whip artists.

Any stuntman or Western stylist who can cut a card in the air or cut a cigarette from someone's mouth has the ability to be a formidable fighter with the whip. He has all the skills that the combat stylist is trying to develop; he just chooses to apply them differently. Since the real difference between the two groups is intent rather than accuracy, control, or precision, the martially inclined would benefit from studying the techniques and methods of safe training used by these performing whip stylists.

The best advice to the beginner is this: wear your safety glasses and hearing protection at all times, follow a clearly defined progression, train that progression as slowly as you need to, and learn from the experiences of others regardless of their foundation in the whip. Last, there is no substitute for personal one-on-one study with an experienced whip handler.

The Latigo y Daga Training Progression

I founded the Latigo y Daga system in 1987 to promote the development of the whip and dagger arts. The term *Latigo y Daga* combines *latigo,* which refers to the leather whip, and *daga,* which is a Filipino term for a short-bladed weapon. In 1987 there were no documented systems of the whip and dagger, so I created the name to promote research into these arts and to identify my system and training method.

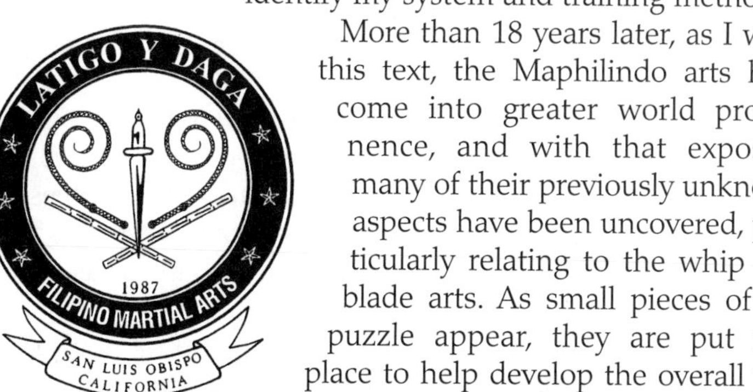

More than 18 years later, as I write this text, the Maphilindo arts have come into greater world prominence, and with that exposure many of their previously unknown aspects have been uncovered, particularly relating to the whip and blade arts. As small pieces of the puzzle appear, they are put into place to help develop the overall picture. It is my sincere hope that, in time, this book and others like it will present a complete picture of the whip and dagger arts.

The Latigo y Daga training method is solidly rooted in Filipino training methodology and principles. The Filipino martial arts are respected all over the world for their effectiveness, which is a direct result of the manner in which they are taught.

One of the first precepts of Filipino combat training is that fundamental movements should apply equally to the stick, blade, and empty hands. This does not mean, as is commonly thought, that everything that works for a stick works for the blade. A blade has an edge, and that edge has to be presented properly for maximum effect. Thus, there are separate bladed techniques that apply, but the fundamental biomechanics of the movements for the stick and blade are the same. In the Filipino arts, the stick is taught first, then bladed weapons, followed by empty hands. This is in contrast to the the majority of the world's martial arts, which teach empty hands first and then progress to weapons training. The Filipino choice of progressive training, and this progression in particular, has a strong logic to it. Stick training can be taught in broad motion groups with simple categories, such as low and high strikes or forehand and backhand strikes. Using these few simple attack angles, the student can then obtain a solid foundation in footwork, angulation, power generation, and whole-body movement. Once the student's basic movement is sound, the strikes are expanded to the whole range of targets on the human body.

Blade work requires precise body movement, which can be taught using the foundation established by the stick basics. Much of what is taught in stick and blade training involves disarming techniques. These techniques instill the basics of locking, throwing, and maintaining centerline. This group of basics then forms the foundation for empty-hand techniques.

These principles of progressive training and motion grouping are at the core of the Latigo y Daga training method. For many years, the biggest obstacle to whip training in these arts has been the physical punishment the student must endure to learn basic techniques. The Latigo y Daga training progression presented in this text is specifically designed to limit accidental injury to the practitioner to an absolute minimum.

The Latigo y Daga whip progression comprises five training blocks:

1. Eskrima basics as they apply to the whip
2. Slashing attacks within the five primary motion groups
3. Cracking the whip
4. Manipulation skills
5. Support weapons for the whip

Each of these training blocks was designed to develop a particular physical skill and to teach the supporting principles for that skill. The skills learned in each block then build on and reinforce one another—in other words, they are progressive. Skipping blocks or learning them out of sequence is counterproductive to your training.

Though it is not possible to entirely eliminate hitting yourself with the whip when you train with it, using a proper instructional progression can minimize it. If you follow the progression offered here, you will achieve maximum results with a minimum of pain or injury.

If you find that you are consistently hitting yourself as you work this progression, it more than likely indicates that you have not properly developed a particular block of skills or that you are practicing the techniques too rapidly and too enthusiastically for your current skill level.

Many whip users are equally comfortable with the right or left hand, and there is no structural difference in learning whip techniques from either the right- or left-handed perspective. The ultimate goal is to be fully ambidextrous with each whip technique and block of material. Each student should choose for himself with which hand to begin his training. However, for purposes of simplification, all of the technical material in this text is presented from the perspective of right-handed whip users.

6

Eskrima Basics

Studying eskrima is a lifetime endeavor, but simply learning certain basic eskrima techniques will provide a working foundation for whip work. These beginning techniques are most easily practiced with a baton or with a whip folded in half and gripped as if it were a baton.

All strikes with the whip can be generally categorized as either forehand or backhand. For a right-handed person, a forehand strike begins with the palm facing away from the body and moves across the body from right to left. A backhand strike begins on the left side of the body, with the palm facing toward the body, and moves from left to right. In the Filipino martial arts, the forehand is often referred to as the open position and the backhand as the closed position. These definitions of forehand and backhand are the same as are used in many sports, such as tennis or racquetball. The terms *forehand, backhand, inward* and *outward palm,* and *open* and *closed positions* will be used extensively in defining striking angles for the whip.

The whip gripped in the folded or "half-whip" position.

The basic forehand or open grip.

The basic backhand or closed grip.

From the forehand and backhand positions, three types of strikes are used: slashing, retracted, and curved. The slashing strike is one that follows through after it makes impact and is most often associated with bladed attacks. The retracted strike, also called a *snap strike* or *jab,* is immediately brought back to the ready position after it makes contact, following the same line from which it is thrown. The curved strike is unique to Filipino stick work and particularly characteristic of the Corto method of Grandmaster Cacoy Canete. This strike is what differentiates Filipino stick manipulation from the "caveman with a club" type of swing. The curved strike comes in on one attack line, but, just before impact, the wielder turns over his wrist, which makes the baton curve into another attack line. This is seen in baseball when a batter turns his wrist over in the same way just after he makes contact with the ball.

The curved strike has many applications for whip users, and it creates some very graceful whip movements. It also is critical to combative applications because it deceives the opponent into expecting an attack on a particular line, when in fact the final point of impact is very different.

Modern eskrima systems use numbered attack lines or angles. There can be as few as five strikes or as many as 64. These techniques can be further broken down into long-, medium-, or close-range applications. The Latigo y Daga system teaches five striking angles as the basic long-range techniques and an additional seven angles when the student moves into the advanced material.

For students familiar with the Filipino martial arts, these first five strikes are known as *cincoteros* (five-count) strikes and are also the same as the first five strikes found in Serrada escrima and Inosanto-LaCoste kali. These five strikes, or attack lines, are as follows:

The number-one striking angle.

The number-two striking angle.

The number-three striking angle.

The number-four striking angle.

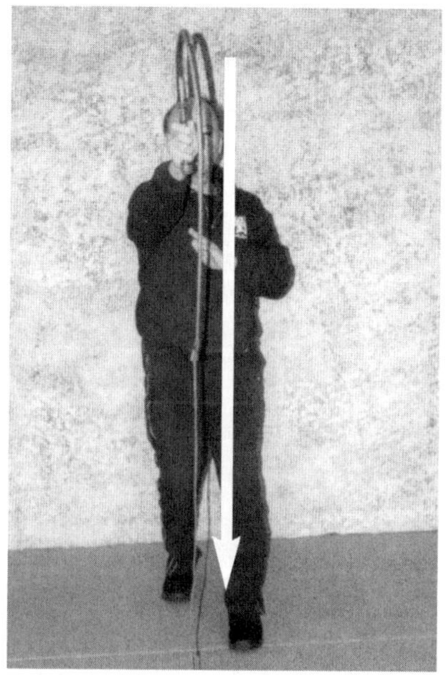

The number-five striking angle from the forehand position.

- Striking angle number one is a downward-diagonal forehand that starts at the opponent's left shoulder and travels to his right hip.
- Striking angle number two is a downward diagonal forehand that starts at the opponent's right shoulder and travels toward his left hip. Note that the palm is facing outward on this strike.
- Striking angle number three is a forehand horizontal strike that begins at the opponent's left waistline and continues through toward his right waistline.
- Striking angle number four is a backhand horizontal strike that begins at the opponent's left waistline and continues through toward his right waistline.

- Striking angle number five is a vertical strike from either the forehand or backhand position that begins at the opponent's head and continues straight down toward his groin.

These striking angles are always the same, whether they are used with slashing, retracted, or curved strikes.

Slashing Attacks with the Whip

When studying the basics with the whip, it is easiest to explore these attack angles as simple slashes. A simple slash does not involve cracking the whip or performing any sophisticated manipulations. It is simply moving the whip as if it were a stick or knife on the described attack line. At this point, the whip is used at its full length, and the skills being developed are the exploration and control of the extension of the whip as it moves through different angles of delivery.

From a combative standpoint, a slash with a whip is every bit as effective as a slash with a knife. A whip slash can cut as easily as a whip crack and does not involve the time delay required to allow the whip to crack.

A concept in the Filipino martial arts called motion grouping has a very profound influence on the study of slashing attacks. Motion grouping means taking any basic attack angle and expanding the range of the simple physical motion involved to cover a greater range of targets. This means that a strike to the head can be seen as the same basic movement as a strike to the neck, and that a strike to the kidneys can be also seen as the same basic movement as a strike to the groin.

With the concept of motion grouping in mind, the five basic attack angles from Latigo y Daga can now be seen to cover a much broader range of targets. If a whip practitioner can accurately strike to the head and then to the waist, he can then use that same motion to attack any other chosen target between the head and the waist. Using this concept, a new striking angle can be defined for each target between the head and waist, depending on how many targets you feel are critical in that area. This choice of critical targets is why some Filipino systems perceive and define as few as five attack angles, or 64 attack angles as in the Pekiti-Tirsia system.

LINE CONTINUATION AND FLOW DRILLS

Line continuation is the process of linking two striking angles together in the most fluid fashion possible. It applies universally whether you are using traditional weapons, the whip, or empty hands, and is the root of flow concepts within the Filipino martial arts. The Filipino flow concept dictates that the physical position at the completion of a technique is the proper biomechanical foundation for the next technique. This eliminates any superfluous repositioning during combat and ensures that the next technique can be presented efficiently and with maximum power.

A perfect example of this type of flow is found in the jab-cross-hook combination of Western boxing: the left jab is thrown and retracted; this retraction movement pushes the right shoulder forward for the cross, and, as the right cross returns, it forces the left hand forward for the hook. This is the utmost in efficiency of movement and embodies all the critical elements of Filipino line continuation.

Applying line continuation at this point in the study means that you must now develop movements that link each of the five

Line continuation of angles one and two showing the figure eight pattern they create when linked together.

basic slashes together in as fluid a manner as possible. One example of this is to take the number-one and number-two slashing angles from Latigo y Daga and link them together in a single continuous movement. You will then find that you are creating a horizontal figure eight in the air in front of you. Rather than letting the whip die at the end of strikes one and two, you are now linking them together in flow and can efficiently connect them in continuous repetition.

Slashes on lines three and four can be as easily linked together in flow by allowing the whip to wrap around your waist on the follow-through of both strikes. What you are doing here is learning to use your body to slow and control the whip on its path. With practice, you will find that the number-three strike will smoothly wrap around the left waistline and the number-four strike will smoothly wrap around the right waistline. This drill

The open-position redondo on the right side of the body.

The closed-position redondo on the left side of the body.

The forehand downward diagonal redondo moving from the right to the left.

must be approached cautiously because too much force can cause the whip to hit you. With practice, you will find that you can do this drill in continuous repetition without injuring yourself.

The vertical number-five striking angle can be added to these line-continuation drills at the end of the number-two or number-four strike. This creates two different striking patterns, the first linking angles 1-2-3-4-5 and the second connecting angles 1-2-5-3-4. You can look at these two basic striking patterns as a drill for training slashes in flow, and once you have explored them, you can create your own patterns just by listing a sequence of the five numbers on paper and seeing how they connect. You will find some combinations that interconnect easily and some that don't.

If some of these combinations of angles don't flow together smoothly at first, it is worth spending the time to explore different manipulation techniques to create a flow for them. This not only increases your whip manipulation skills, but may also open avenues of study and research you might not find otherwise.

Steve Kohn, a certified Latigo y Daga instructor, has developed a unique method of resolving line-continuation issues. When a line does not flow from left to right, Steve will simply hand off the whip to the free hand and smoothly continue the line from the other side of the body. This is an important area of study and exploration because it significantly improves flow and helps develop ambidextrous whip skills. This improved flow aids significantly in training with other weapons and the empty hands as well.

At this point, we are still only slashing with the whip; we are not actively attempting to crack it. Occasionally during these drills the whip may crack of its own accord, but it is important to remember that what you are focusing on is developing sensitivity to the whip as it extends itself around your body. Once you have developed a foundation for this sensitivity, you can more easily learn actual whip-cracking skills.

Now that you have a working understanding of motion grouping and line analysis as they apply to whip-slashing techniques, you can explore the redondo motion groups of the Filipino martial arts. The term *redondo* refers to the rotary motion that creates circular patterns of movement with the weapon being used.

Five redondo motions apply to basic whip training:

1. The forehand (open) redondo on the right side of the body
2. The backhand (closed) redondo on the left side of the body

The backhand downward diagonal redondo moving from the left to right.

The overhead redondo. This movement closely resembles the blades of a helicopter as they spin around; in fact, in both Momoy Canete's whip system and Latigo y Daga, this technique is called the helicopter movement.

3. The forehand downward diagonal redondo moving from the right to the left
4. The forehand (palm out) downward diagonal redondo moving from the left to right
5. The overhead redondo

These methods can be practiced in both the clockwise and counterclockwise directions. At the basic level, however, it is best to simplify the training and practice the movements in the clockwise, or forward, direction. These movements are easy to practice individually and, just like the basic first five strikes, can be linked together in continuous flow. The easiest pattern to start with is the 1-5-2 redondo pattern. These motions link very easily and can be followed with redondo motions 5-1 to create a 1-5-2-5-1 pattern, which is a nonstop flow drill.

The next pair of movements to practice is the 3-4 redondo pair; these movements will link effortlessly with just a little practice. This 3-4 flow can now be added to the 1-5-2-5-1 redondo flow for a simple drill that combines all five of the basic redondo movements into a single linked movement.

This process of combining angles to create training drills is called the application-of-line variables. Exploring line variables is the easiest and most thorough means of examining all possible options when using a whip. Line variables will become increasingly more important as you develop the ability to crack the whip.

Cracking the Whip

Once you understand the laws of physics that govern whip cracking, you must then learn to apply proper technique to complement these laws most efficiently. Observation of whip users reveals as many seemingly different ways to crack a whip as there are users. No matter how they throw the whip to make it crack, they all have this in common: their motion straightens the whip out, and this process accelerates the popper to its peak velocity. It is at this velocity that the popper breaks the sound barrier.

One of the reasons for the Latigo y Daga emphasis on the redondo movements for whip work is that they make it easy to straighten the whip out during its throw. If you have successfully developed basic redondo slashing skills, you will have already cracked the whip numerous times as an incidental by-product of changing slashing lines. These cracks are normal because when you change from one slashing line to another, the whip straightens out as it changes direction or angle. As you reverse directions within any given redondo movement, the whip will also straighten out and crack.

The redondo motion is unique in that it also allows the user to crack the whip without any directional change at all. With the whip traveling in an arc around the body, all the user must do is pause momentarily in the movement and the whip will straighten out and crack. The user needs to pause for only a fraction of a second to initiate the straightening process. At the pause, the whip will crack and continue along in the exact same arc it began on. From a combative standpoint, the pause is nearly invisible to the opponent, which makes it very difficult for him to establish the point of an incoming attack.

Many whip users pull the whip back toward themselves when cracking it, and this is one way to get it to straighten out. However, from the Latigo y Daga perspective, this is the most dangerous thing you can do with a whip because it will pull the whip directly into your body or face. This style of whip cracking is highly dangerous and greatly increases the chance of injury to yourself when you apply it.

From a technical standpoint, there is absolutely no need to pull a whip back to get it to crack, and, generally, the whip will go slack on the pullback, thus requiring wasted movements to get the whip back into motion. The whole process of using the pullback motion is also noticeably slower than using redondo motions. The pullback technique also puts an enormous physical strain on the whip and tends to destroy the knot where the fall connects to the thong. For these reasons, there are no pullback techniques in the material presented here.

GRIPPING THE WHIP

The grip used to hold a whip can strongly influence the manipulation required to get it to crack. In the Latigo y Daga method, there are nine basic grips used for the whip:

1. Holding the thong above the upper knob
2. Holding on the upper knob

3. Holding the center of the grip
4. Holding the lower knob in the palm of the hand
5. Cradling the lower knob between the index and second fingers in the V-grip
6. Holding the lower knob in the palm of the hand with the whip handle inverted
7. Holding the center of the grip with the whip handle inverted
8. Holding the upper knob with the whip handle inverted
9. Holding below the upper knob with the whip handle inverted

---

This photo sequence demonstrates the nine basic grips used in Latigo y Daga.

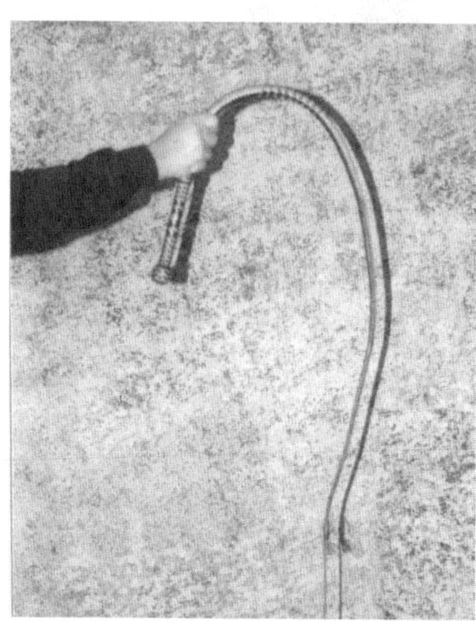

Holding the thong above the upper knob.

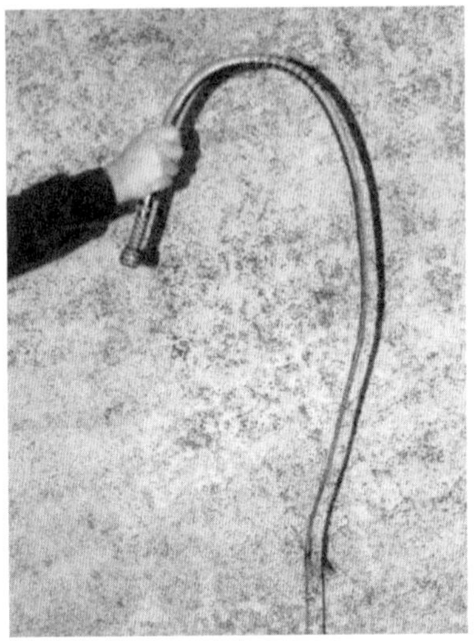

Holding onto the upper knob.

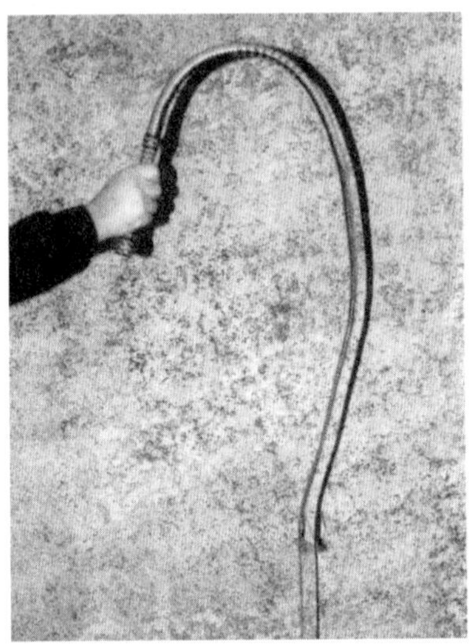

Holding the center of the grip.

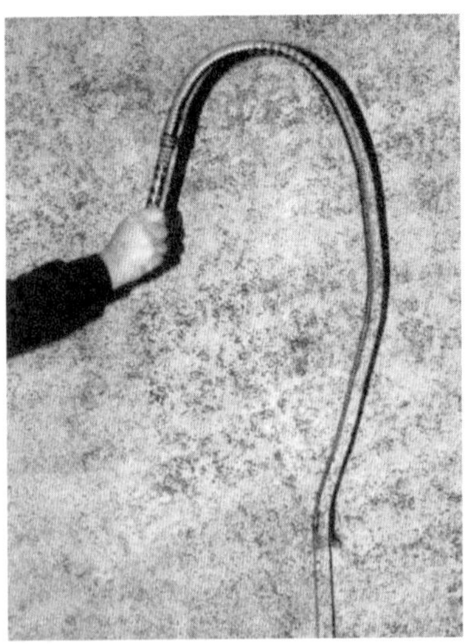

Holding the lower knob in the palm of the hand.

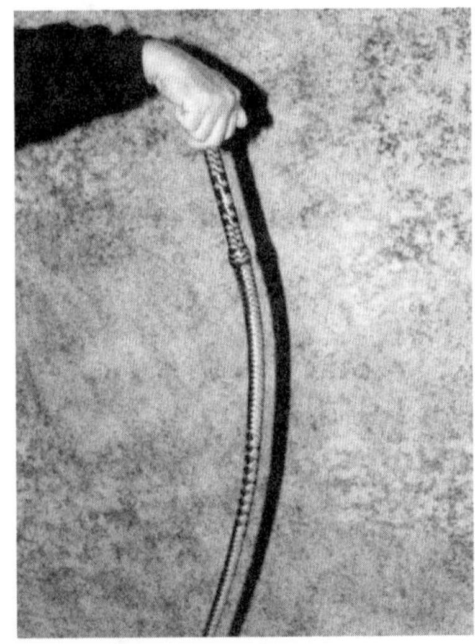

Cradling the lower knob between the index and second fingers in the V-grip.

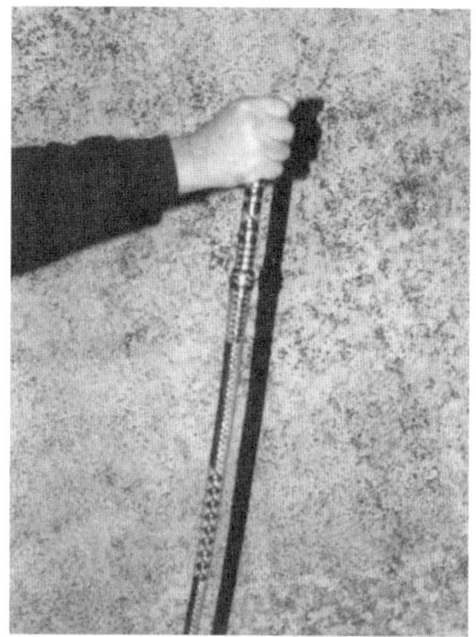

Holding the lower knob in the palm of the hand with the whip handle inverted.

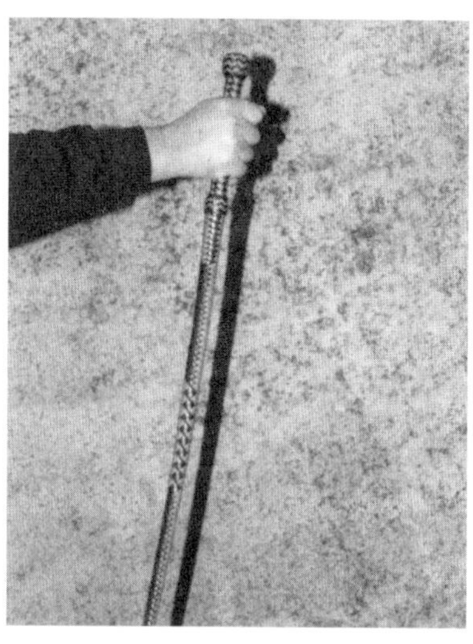

Holding the center of the grip with the whip handle inverted.

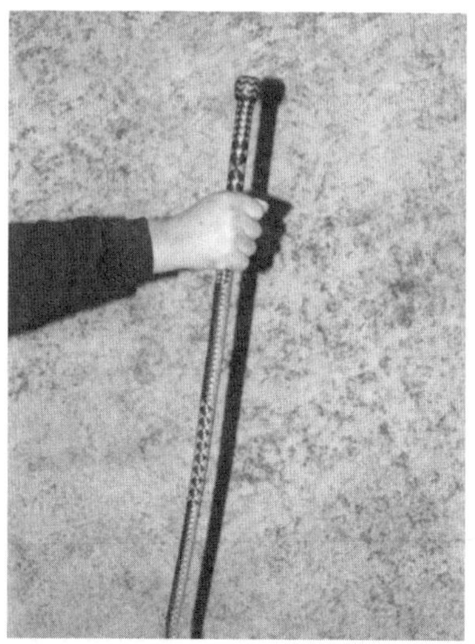

Holding the upper knob with the whip handle inverted.

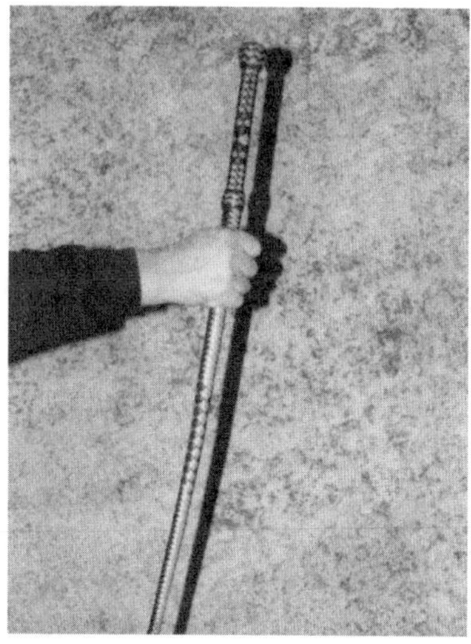

Holding below the upper knob with the whip handle inverted.

For a basic study of whip cracking, the two most important grips are the handle and the lower-knob grips. The handle grip is the easiest to begin with, but sometimes using the lower-knob grip will remove the wrist action from the equation, which helps to troubleshoot problems in whip cracking.

ALIGNING THE WHIP FOR CRACKING

The whip must be properly aligned with itself for smooth, effortless cracking. There are two fundamental positions in which to hold the whip to control its alignment during the throw—self-aligned and inverted—and the chosen alignment position has a profound effect on how the whip moves when it is thrown and cracked.

When the whip is held out horizontally from the body, it assumes a downward curve. As it is rotated in the hand and around its own axis, it becomes apparent that this curve can change considerably in shape and size. Generally the whip will exhibit two dominant curves: a large bend in one position and, after rotating the whip 180 degrees in the hand, a much smaller bend. This characteristic, found in most whips, is because of the way the belly of the whip is tightened during the braiding process.

The large bend occurs when the whip is in perfect alignment with itself for the most efficient transmission of energy. This is called the *self-aligned position*. When the whip is rotated 180 degrees, it assumes the smaller bend, called the *inverted position*. When held in the self-aligned position, the whip maintains a full loop on itself as it rolls out. This full loop will travel down the length of the thong until the whip cracks. This causes the whip to follow a very smooth, clean arc until it cracks and is in fact the most efficient use of a whip's design. In the inverted position, the thong of the whip does not cross over itself when thrown, and it actually moves in the shape of an S prior to cracking. This

The whip held in the self-aligned position.

The whip held in the inverted-alignment position.

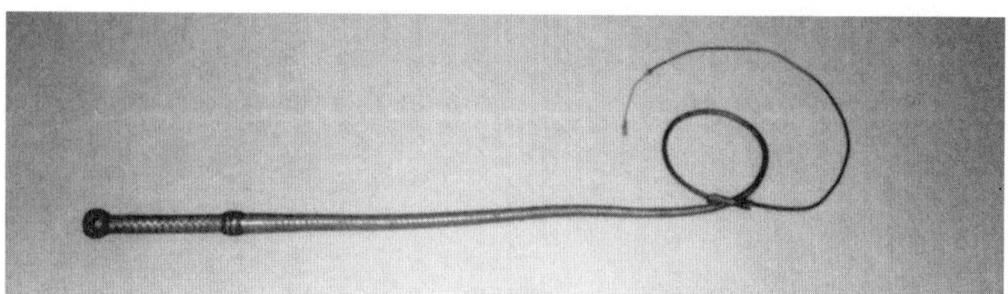

The shape assumed by the whip when it is thrown from the self-aligned position.

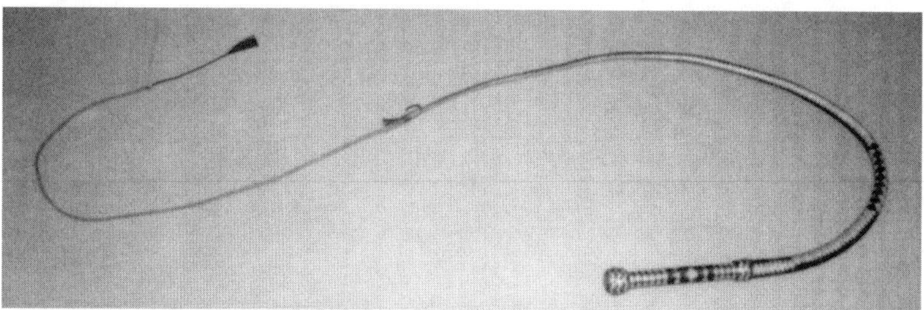

The shape assumed by the whip when it is thrown from the inverted-alignment position.

alignment allows the whip to be cracked very close to the body and, in general, permits faster cracking.

Proper use of the self-aligned position, and the subsequent smooth roll, is the hallmark of the "follow the handle," rolling style developed by Anthony DeLongis. After observing countless whip manipulators overwork their whips, DeLongis began to develop a style that would take advantage of the whip's own physical structure to achieve effortless alignment. The heart of this style lies in holding the whip in the self-aligned position, which he refers to as "rolling the whip above the handle." The whip user then pushes the handle, rather than throwing it, which pulls the thong into the looped position. This loop then rolls down the length of the whip, just like water flowing downhill. In DeLongis' own words: "By employing this simple adjust-

Anthony DeLongis demonstrates the signature loop that results from using his method of aligning the whip.

ment, the whip is able to form the critical alignment loop much earlier in the throw. The whip requires much less energy to produce the crack because it uses its own structural alignment to create energy more quickly and efficiently. Consider for a moment: Water runs downhill. Why push water uphill so that it can run back down that same hill? That's the simple advantage to my system: ease, efficiency, and consistency."

In 2002 a study called "The Shape of a Cracking Whip" was published in *The American Physical Society* to extensively analyze the energy generated by a cracking whip. The study concluded that the loop generated by DeLongis' technique is in fact the most efficient way to crack a whip.

Professionals in the Hollywood film industry favor DeLongis' method because it provides exceptional camera visibility and displays a remarkable level of grace when done properly. As DeLongis explains, "My style prolongs the visual moment as long as possible and gives the maximum time for storytelling with the whip." Equally important to the way the whip is held is the overall body alignment that DeLongis uses. This body alignment creates astonishing accuracy and control, and provides a complete zone of safety for performers on the set. His training methods for using the whip are second to none. Any student with a serious interest in whip techniques will benefit greatly from studying the DeLongis method.

Latigo y Daga techniques can be executed quite effectively using either alignment. Most of the techniques in this book were developed using the inverted alignment, principally because the need for high manipulation speed is of greater combative value than the pursuit of absolute mechanical efficiency of the whip.

Students exploring Latigo y Daga techniques should experiment with both alignments since each has its own strengths and weaknesses.

Steve Kohn, a student of the DeLongis method and an instructor of Latigo y Daga, sees the balance this way: "Anthony wants you to see everything as it happens; Tom wants you to feel it before you see it. Everything Anthony does is wholly aesthetic; everything Tom does is totally ballistic."

FOREHAND VERTICAL CRACK

The forehand vertical crack is one of the easiest cracking lines to learn and provides an excellent foundation for learning others. Students of the Western whip arts know this crack as the "gypsy" or "lion tamer's" crack. In the Filipino martial arts, it is described as a forehand vertical crack done on the right side of the body, and it can also be executed in continuous repetition using the forehand redondo movement.

In the forehand vertical crack, the user begins the motion by laying out the whip behind him on the right side; pulling the whip forward until it straightens out in front; and, when the whip is at full forward extension, pulling it up and back until it is behind his shoulder. He then throws it forward and downward to the rear on the exact line on which it began. The whip describes a 270-degree arc both as it is brought up and as it is thrown forward.

To get the whip to crack during this motion, all you need to do is pause momentarily at the point you wish it to crack. This pause allows the whip to straighten out, at which point it stops its forward motion and cracks. At the beginning stages of training, you should exaggerate this momentary pause until the whip visibly begins to straighten out, at which point you can halt the entire motion or allow the throw to continue back to its starting point. The point at which the pause is initiated ultimately determines the direction and focus of the whip crack.

This point of pause is very similar to the point of release used when throwing a knife or baseball. When throwing the whip, you should visualize the desired target point in front of you and time the pause so that the whip cracks as it passes the target point. With extensive practice, you will develop these focus and

Using a short whip, LaVonne Martin demonstrates the loop formation that occurs when the forehand vertical crack is thrown from the self-aligned position.

Note that the thong of the whip is to the rear of Martin's hand and outside of her arm. This begins the formation of the loop.

Pushing her arm and wrist forward, Martin creates the loop above the handle.

The whip moves this loop down its length until the end of the throw. The whip fully straightens out as it makes the popper crack. After it cracks, it continues smoothly forward and downward. The quality of LaVonne's throw can be seen here in the smooth curve maintained by the whip as it continues forward.

timing skills quite rapidly and will eventually be able to crack the whip at any point in the 270-degree arc when you add the pause. You can crack the whip as it is pulled to the lower rear, as it is pulled to the front, as it is pulled to the upper rear, and finally as it is thrown forward for the basic forehand crack. This gives four cracks in the 270-degree arc of travel.

Once you master the basic single-forehand crack, the next step is to learn to crack the whip as it executes the full 360-degree forehand-redondo movement. The forehand redondo is spun just as you have practiced it; the only difference is that there is now a pause as the whip passes in front of you. The whip will crack, and you will then continue the redondo circle on around. Each time the whip passes in front of you, you make it crack again. You can do this drill with a crack on every revolution, or you can mix the cracks with noncracking slashes in any sequence or combination desired. This redondo-based foundation allows you to crack the whip on any of the redondo lines repeatedly and with no interruption of the circular movement.

You can now see that the basic redondo angles are the line continuation of the first five strikes in Latigo y Daga system. You can use the redondo movement in flow to continuously crack the whip on all five of the Latigo y Daga attack angles simply by changing the angle of the rotary motion.

When you are continuously cracking the whip on the number-two forehand line, you may experience some difficulty because of the natural tendency to change from the forehand to a backhand as the whip comes around the left side of body. Just be sure that the palm is always facing outward when executing this throw to help you get the timing right for the pause.

With these changes in angle, you must do some extra manipulation to clear your head and body because of the whip's pausing and cracking in its path. You will develop these manipulation skills to some degree when practicing the slashing basics and improve them with further practice.

FREE-HAND CONTROL OF THE WHIP

The weaponless hand in the Filipino martial arts is commonly referred to as the free hand, the live hand, or the third hand. Free-hand techniques vary greatly from style to style and, in most cases, are among the defining differences between styles. The free hand can be used to control an opponent's weapon, redirect his body, or execute locking techniques. The number of options for using the free hand in the martial arts is virtually limitless. In whip training the position of the free hand works as a balance to the pull and mass of the whip at extension and thus is critical to sound technique. Combative applications require a high degree of sophistication in positioning the free hand to aid the subtle shifting of balance that occurs during high-speed multiple crackings.

The free hand is used extensively to control the whip with the cracking applications of the number-three and -four attack angles. These applications cannot be executed correctly without the use of the free hand, and the basic skills developed here will become the foundation for a whole range of advanced free-hand techniques with the whip. The most basic freehand position used in whip manipulation in long range is the palm-rearward position, with the left arm kept in a relaxed position next to the body.

Cracking the whip on the number-three and -four lines uses the same basic motion as in slashing, but you now add the pause and your free hand controls the thong of the whip. In the basic slashing drill, you allowed your body to control the wrap of the whip as it swung around your waist. Since you are now cracking the whip, the energy level is higher, requiring you to use your left arm and hand to maintain control of the whip.

The following is the proper sequence used to crack the whip on the number-three line:

- Throw the whip horizontally in front and pause just as it passes the midpoint. The whip will crack and continue toward the left side.
- Hold your left arm down and extended about a foot in front of the body, with the palm facing rearward. Catch the thong of the whip just above the back of the hand at the wrist line.
- Do not stop the whip with your arm and wrist, but gently meet it and guide it to the rear. The whip stops at rest on top of the left hand, which is now relaxed and held in alignment with the left leg.
- Rotate the left hip toward the rear simultaneously with the arm motion. This synchronizes the whip, the free hand and arm, and the hip rotation into a single, graceful motion.

It is important to fully develop the skills of the free-hand catch for the number-three strike before moving on to cracking the whip on the number-four line. This is because positioning the hips rearward, with the whip resting on top of the free hand, is the required posture from which to launch the number-four strike.

The number-four strike begins with the whip at rest on top of the left hand, where it finished after the number-three throw. The left hand and hip then simultaneously move forward to begin the whip's horizontal acceleration forward. As the hip approaches a more neutral position, push the hand forward of the body to give some added velocity to the whip during the throw. Approximately 30 percent of the impetus of the throw should come from the free hand.

When the strike is complete, the hand will finish where it began, approximately 1 foot in front of the body. Pause the whip again as it passes the centerline; after it cracks, allow it to continue around to wrap around your right waist and rear. From this position, you can launch the whip again into the number-three line.

Latigo y Daga angle number three.

Throw the whip horizontally from the right.

Extend the left hand to catch the whip.

Catch the whip on the back of the left hand.

The hand continues to the rear of the body to a point of rest.

Latigo y Daga angle number four.

The throw begins with the whip resting on the left hand, which is held to the rear of the body.

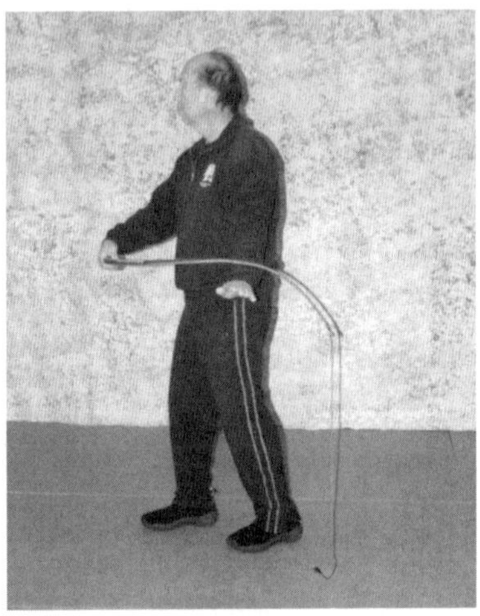

Both the hand and left hip come forward, and the whip begins to lose contact with the hand.

The whip continues across the front.

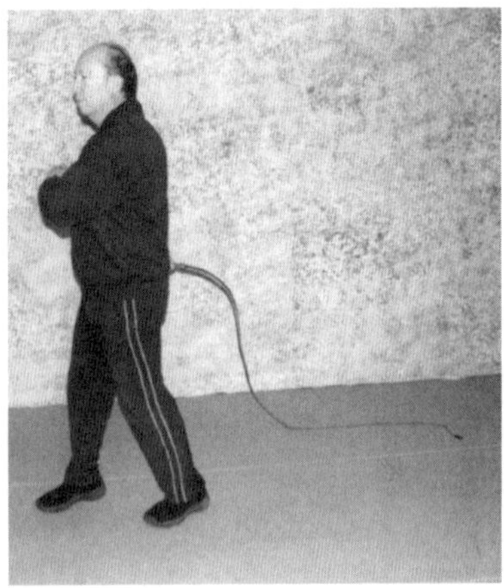

The whip finishes at rest around the right side of the body.

The number-three and -four lines can now be practiced together in flow. These two cracking lines are the most difficult to develop and require considerably more time to master than any of the other strikes.

9 Whip Manipulation Drills

Now that you have acquired working skills in cracking and slashing with the whip on all five attack lines, it is now time to explore the creation of different line variables. When you combine strikes in any given pattern, you create a line variable. If you execute the first five Latigo y Daga strikes in a sequential 1-2-3-4-5 pattern, you have executed just one of many possible line variables. You can reverse this drill and strike 5-4-3-2-1 for another line variable. Writing out the line variables when exploring them ensures that you have a record of what you have done, and you can note any pattern that flows particularly well.

One of the most fundamental drills in the Latigo y Daga system is to explore all the double-striking line variables possible using the five basic striking angles. The numbers used in the following chart are the same as the striking angles of the basic Latigo y Daga strikes.

As you practice these line variables, you will note five redondo pairs that you have already practiced: 1-1, 2-2, 3-3, 4-4, and

1-1	2-1	3-1	4-1	5-1
1-2	2-2	3-2	4-2	5-2
1-3	2-3	3-3	4-3	5-3
1-4	2-4	3-4	4-4	5-4
1-5	2-5	3-5	4-5	5-5

This chart lists the 25 paired strikes possible using the line-variables approach.

5-5. You can also use these redondo skills to find flow solutions to other line variables.

In exploring line variables, it is important to mix up slashes with cracks, speed changes, different footwork, and other techniques you wish to investigate. Every technique or positioning change you include will increase the range and diversity of your whip skills. The possibilities are endless and can provide you with a broad canvas for expressing your creativity.

FOOTWORK

There are three fundamental ways to stand when throwing a whip, and each has a distinct influence on the control of the whip. The first stance is the forward position, with both the weapon and leading foot forward of the body; the second option is to stand with both feet parallel; and the third choice is to stand in the retracted position, which puts the weapon arm to the rear of the leading foot. Whip stylists who prefer to use the elbow

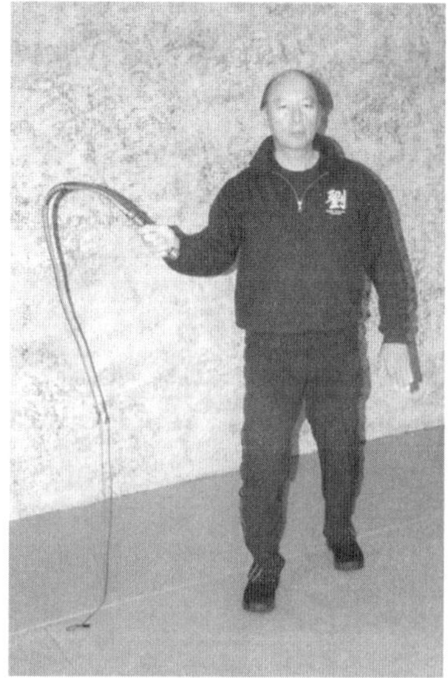

The forward stance.

and shoulder alignment to control the whip use the retracted position. This position provides a very solid base for the upper body, which keeps the arm and elbow in better alignment during the throw.

The parallel stance is most common for target work because it allows the user to make slight range adjustments by leaning forward or backward or twisting side to side during the throw. This works well for some people, but it can easily cause you to become off balance, par-

The parallel stance.

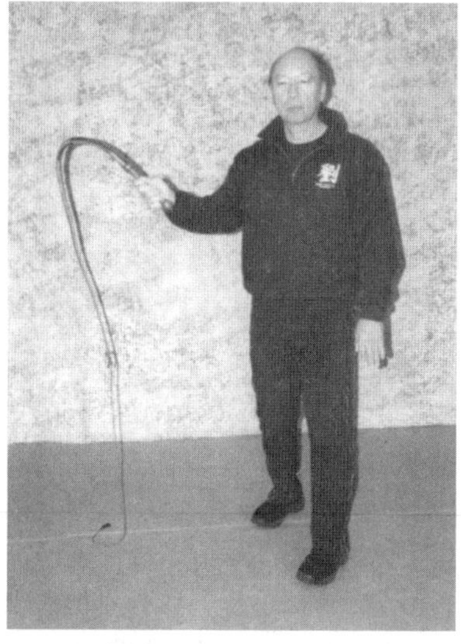

The retracted stance.

ticularly if you are using a heavy whip. This loss of balance clearly affects combative applications, and the parallel stance is best used as a transitional stance between whip strikes.

The forward position is used in Latigo y Daga for long-range techniques for two reasons: it gives the greatest range possible with the whip; and, by positioning the leg opposite the weapon to the rear, that leg is less likely to interfere with the whip during the large redondo motions.

The drawback to the normal whip-forward position is that the arm and extended whip create a very long, flexible lever, which can easily pull the arm and body out of alignment and balance during the throw. This can force the body out of the correct position for the next throw. Careful attention to the position of the arm and alignment of the whip helps to minimize this problem.

Any of the flow drills can be done with normal or retracted footwork or with any combination of strikes, slashes, and footwork changes. The five basic strikes should now be done using both the normal and retracted footwork to examine the range shifts that occur. All the redondo groups should be reexamined to see how the change in footwork influences the proximity of the whip to the body.

The simplest and most effective way to explore footwork is to practice striking with the whip while walking forward 10 steps and then turning around and taking 10 steps back, all while striking with the whip. This integrates striking, footwork, and body positioning into a unified movement, which is necessary for working combatively in all directions.

QUADRANT TRAINING

In Latigo y Daga, there are four combative quadrants in which to train. If you stand in the center of a circle, the four quadrants are 90 degrees apart and are numbered one, two,

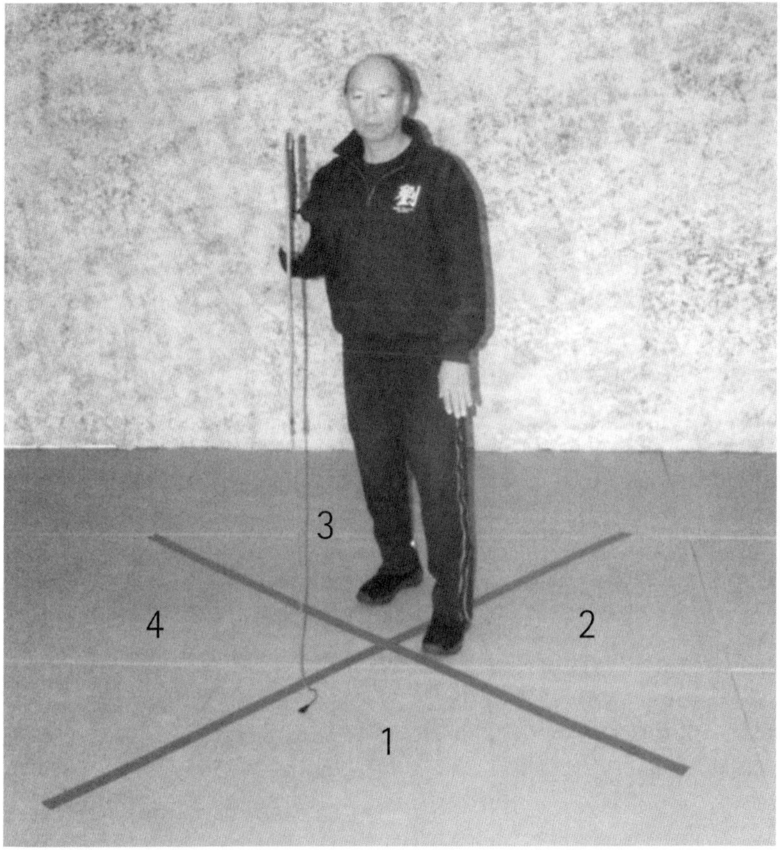

Professor Ron Lew demonstrates the correct base position to practice the use of the quadrants. Their respective numbers identify the quadrants.

three, and four in a counterclockwise direction. The goal of training in these quadrants is to learn how to maneuver from one quadrant to another while maintaining combative flow of the whip. Successful quadrant training provides the necessary skills to deal with an attack from the front, rear, or sides.

Line continuation becomes critical in quadrant training because you are now allowing the pull and alignment of the whip to determine the direction your body turns. When you strike with the whip, you are no longer changing the whip's path to clear your body but are instead moving your body out of the path of the whip. The body now turns with the whip as it moves to the left, right, or toward the rear. One of the goals at this stage is to develop natural footwork patterns that synchronize the body's turning movements with the whip's line extension.

The four quadrants can be viewed as both physical zones and time intervals. The duration of a whip throw can change considerably with any turning motion. A strike thrown in quadrant one, followed by a strike in quadrant two, takes a shorter amount of time than if the second strike was in quadrant three. You can apply this principle in your training to extend the time between strikes in order to better feel the extension of the whip in the air.

All the skills developed up to this point should be practiced in transition from one quadrant to another. You can create basic quadrant drills using slashes or cracks or any combination of the first five Latigo y Daga striking angles. You can mix these angles with other line variables to create your own flow drills, just as with the line-variable drills used in other stages of training.

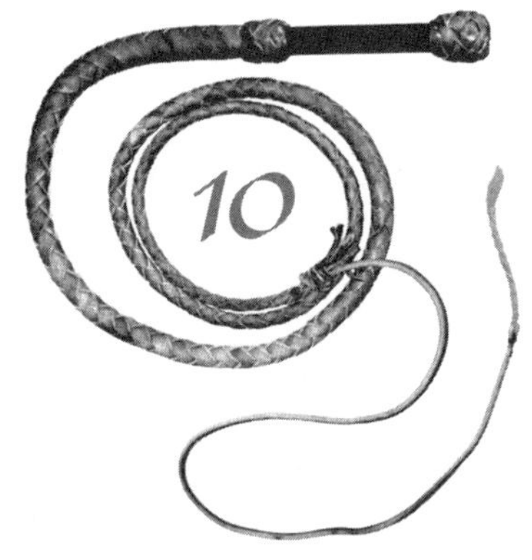

Support Weapons with the Whip

A wide range of weapons can be used to support a whip, including another whip, a baton, or a dagger. The dagger is highly effective and is an ideal choice for students new to the use of tandem weapons. The dagger is short enough not to tangle the whip and is used extensively in many Filipino systems as a secondary weapon.

Espada y daga (sword and dagger) techniques are found in many Filipino systems. These traditional techniques, and particularly those used by Grandmaster Cacoy Canete of the Doce Pares system, form the foundation for the whip and dagger work found in the Latigo y Daga system.

The overall range of Filipino espada y daga techniques is great enough to warrant a separate course of study, and this should be augmented with a study of Italian and Spanish rapier and dagger techniques. Anthony DeLongis' skills in European sword and dagger work are as exceptional as his whip work, and any student interested in further research in this area would be well advised to pursue training with him in these techniques.

Whip and dagger work requires a different synchronization from that used with the stick and dagger or sword and dagger. This is because of both the length of the whip, which changes the range and extends the time interval, and the flexibility of the whip, which can cause it to tangle with the dagger. At the beginning levels of support weapon training, it is easiest to practice the techniques with a baton or whip in the folded position. Once the timing and synchronization of the movements are developed with a rigid weapon, it becomes easier to introduce the whip with its greater flexibility and range of movement.

The mechanics of the free-hand techniques learned earlier now come into play to both control the whip and extend the knife forward of the whip. The basic synchronization of the whip and dagger consists of extending the knife as the whip comes rearward and retracting the knife as the whip goes forward. With the knife in hand, it becomes important to not touch the whip with the blade or cut your own arm and hand as they pass by.

The following patterns show how the Latigo y Daga strikes can be synchronized with the dagger. These basic patterns can be practiced as individual techniques or linked together in flow. Always use a suitable training knife when practicing these techniques.

Attack Angle Number One

Hold the whip at rest on the right side of the body and retract the dagger level with the left shoulder. Throw the whip from the right to the left. As the whip passes the center of the user's body, the dagger begins to come forward and stops at full extension on the centerline of the opponent's face. The whip should wrap around the user's waist just as the dagger is at full extension.

The beginning point for angle number one supported with the dagger.

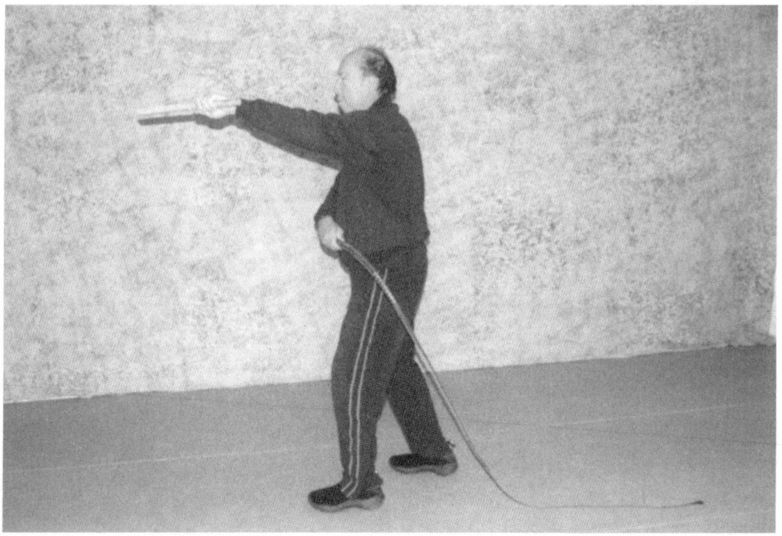

The finishing point for angle number one.

Attack Angle Number Two

The whip is now low and outside the dagger on the user's left side. As the whip comes up into angle two, retract the dagger to the shoulder in order to clear the whip. As soon as the whip clears the dagger, thrust the dagger forward on a downward angle, slightly trailing the angle-two whip strike. The knife stops at the opponent's kidney line, and the whip continues toward the right and flows into the number-three strike angle. It is important to keep the whip completely in the air during the transition from the number-two angle to the number-three angle.

The beginning point for angle number two supported with the dagger.

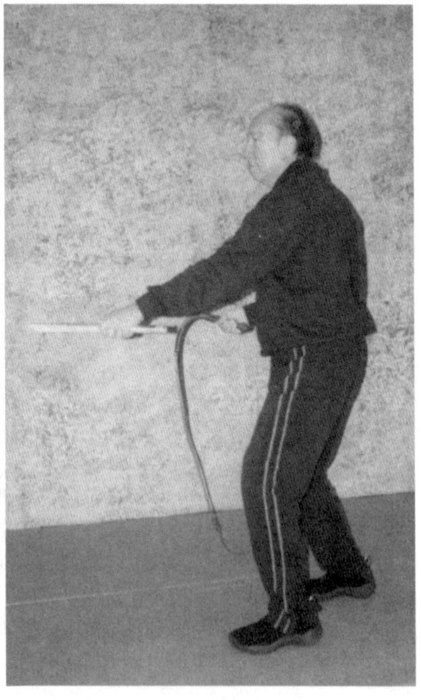

The finishing point for angle number two.

Attack Angle Number Three

As you throw the whip to the left, retract the dagger and hold it horizontally at the waistline with the wrist bent slightly upward. Catch the whip on top of the wrist as you rotate the wrist and hips rearward. Do not allow the whip to contact the knife or the knife to touch you.

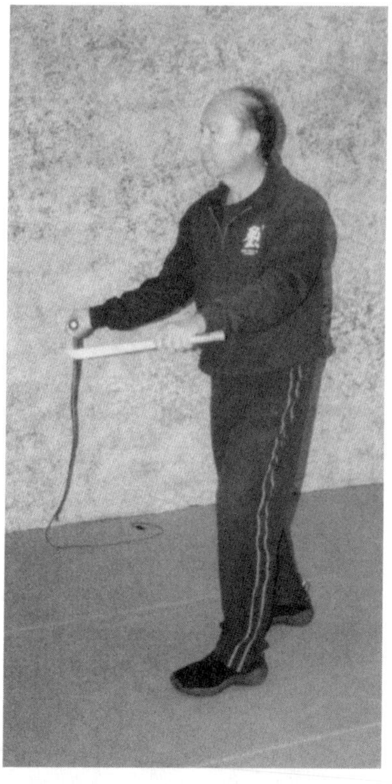

The beginning point for angle number three supported with the dagger.

The finishing point for angle number three.

Attack Angle Number Four

Thrust the dagger and the whip forward using hip rotation to create momentum. Pull the whip forward and to the right ahead of the dagger and allow the dagger to follow the whip forward to the opponent's kidney.

The beginning point for angle number four supported with the dagger.

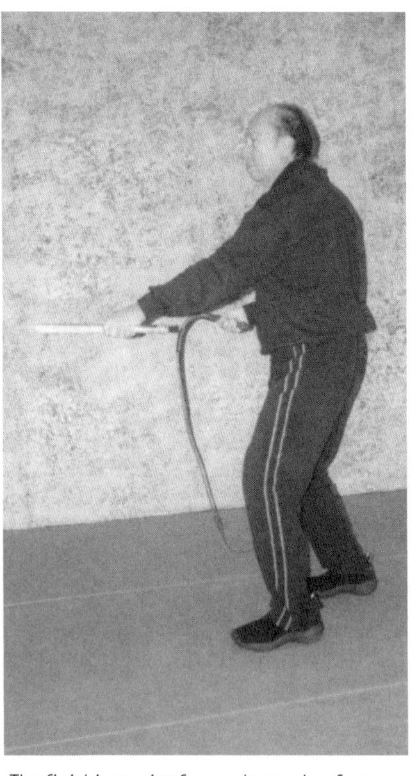

The finishing point for angle number four.

Attack Angle Number Five

As the whip comes across to the right, bring it around to the rear and move it upward from the rear and then downward in the front as a vertical strike to the opponent's face. As the strike comes downward, retract the dagger high and to the left to clear the whip. The whip continues down and under your right arm. This clears the line for the dagger, which you then thrust to the opponent's face.

The beginning point for angle number five supported with the dagger.

The finishing point for angle number five.

You should practice these basic patterns of synchronization very slowly until they are fully integrated into the body. At that point, increase the speed of the drill until the movements degrade and the whip begins to tangle with the body or the dagger. Then reduce the speed to a level where you can control it. Repeating this process will ultimately allow you to progress to a full-speed integration of the dagger thrusts with the whip strikes.

There are numerous other patterns for the whip and dagger that you can use, but do not approach them until you have established a solid foundation in these basic patterns. You can find advanced patterns in espada y daga techniques or generate them yourself by using the principles presented in the study of line variables.

11 Training with the Traditional Doce Pares Rope Whip

The Doce Pares Club is one of the oldest and most respected eskrima associations in the Philippines. The club was founded in 1932 by the top-ranking Cebuano eskrimadors of the day, which included members of the Saavedras family and the Canete brothers. At the time of the club's inception, Filemon "Momoy" Canete was considered one of the top fighters of the time. Momoy's primary specialty in Doce Pares was his espada y daga techniques. He was very broad-based in his technical abilities and was one of the few Doce Pares grandmasters to integrate the whip into his system. By trade, Momoy was a rope maker, and he braided his own whips out of the rope he made. His whips were 6 to 8 feet long with a 15-inch wooden handle and would be classified as a type of stock whip.

The Doce Pares Club has a growing international membership under the current head of the system, Grandmaster Ciriaco "Cacoy" Canete. Grandmaster Canete is truly one of the greatest living eskrimadors; he is the Doce Pares Club champion and has

Grandmaster Cacoy Canete with the author.

fought more than 100 challenge fights without a single loss, over a span of 48 years.

I have had the great fortune to train with Grandmaster Canete since 1990, and many of the practical applications in this text were learned the hard way, at the end of Grandmaster Cacoy's baton, just as he learned his lessons from the baton of his elder brother, Momoy Canete.

At the age of 5, Momoy took the young Cacoy under his wing and began his training in the Filipino martial arts. Grandmaster Cacoy credits Momoy with developing in him much of the toughness needed to win every fight he fought. The young Cacoy was Momoy's training partner for many years, which meant that he inevitably took the brunt of the punishment as Momoy explored new techniques.

When Momoy began his exploration of the whip during World War II, Cacoy once again served as Momoy's training partner for the development of new techniques, particularly Momoy's whip-disarming techniques against the baton and knife. Grandmaster Cacoy still vividly recalls those training sessions: "When we were done, I could see the coil of lash marks all over my hand from his technique."

In 1991, when Momoy Canete was 80 years old, Richard Hudson trained with him for 6 months in the Philippines. Of his impression when he saw Momoy use the whip for the first time, Hudson recalls, "It was awesome, fascinating. I had never seen or thought of the Filipinos using the whip."

The author with Grandmaster Momoy Canete.

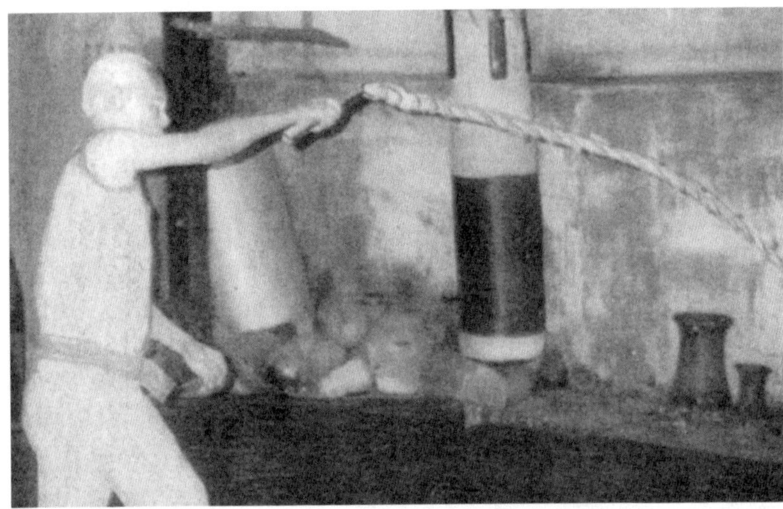

Grandmaster Momoy Canete demonstrates the use of the rope whip.

Richard Hudson in Los Angeles at the 2001 Doce Pares Invitational Tournament.

Hudson is a very successful full-contact eskrima fighter and a dedicated practitioner of the Doce Pares system, and he clearly recalls this training: "Grandmaster Momoy taught a range of weapons and empty-hand techniques. He liked to teach combat judo and taught double axes, pressure points, and the palm stick as well. He also taught throwing knife techniques that were developed for the assassination of Japanese collaborators. He would refer to these techniques as 'truly silent death.'"

Hudson notes that after each training session Momoy would tell them to "go home and practice these techniques." One of the few students who took this advice, Hudson believes that this extra practice allowed him to develop a greater degree of flow and sensitivity of the basic whip strikes in about two weeks.

Grandmaster Momoy's whip techniques were primarily throws pulled back just prior to the point of impact, which would cause the whip to crack in a very linear fashion directly on the target. He used the whip in something akin to a fencing style, with the whip being thrown with the lead leg forward.

Hudson recalls that targeting with the whip was taught from the very beginning: "Grandmaster Momoy would start by attacking the ankles, then the knees, and work his way on up to the head. This allowed the student to pick a target and develop flow in attacking the chosen target."

Grandmaster Momoy used his experience as a rope maker to make his own whips, and he liked to knot the whip heavily throughout its taper. Hudson recalls: "His whip was heavy; it really worked you. It had knots all up and down its length. When I first started, I kept cracking the whip behind me until I got the timing and sensitivity right. When I first began learning the whip, I would hit myself in the back, and those knots really hurt."

Grandmaster Momoy had several unique applications with the whip. These included holding the handle of the whip in one hand and gripping a loop of the whip with the other, while the lash of the whip hung nearly to the ground. This allowed the use of the handle for *punio* (butt) strikes, the loop for grappling, and still kept the lash free to use as a short whip. Releasing the loop would bring the full 8-foot length of the whip back into play.

Hudson feels that he got many rewards from his whip training with Grandmaster Momoy and recommends whip training for martial artists: "I think whip training should be included in a student's training. They should do this, and more of the Filipino martial arts, for a wider perspective."

Hudson's experience is similar to that of Grandmaster "Bo" Sayoc, who trained with Momoy Canete in 1976 and 1978. He returned from the Philippines with what was described by his son,

The author demonstrates the smooth rollout of the rope whip.

Tuhon Chris Sayoc, as "extraordinary video footage" of Momoy's whip work. The son also commented that Momoy's footwork couldn't be explained on paper. The Sayoc clan has one of the longest-standing traditions of using the whip within their kali system, and the Sayoc knife fighting system is considered one of the best and most complete in the world. They have integrated this material with the whip and have some unique whip and dagger techniques not found in any other system. There are currently 19 instructors certified to teach the Sayoc whip curriculum.

Guro Dan Inosanto is a longtime friend of Grandmaster "Bo" Sayoc, and he credits the Sayoc family for a portion of his whip training. I learned many of Guro Inosanto's whip techniques and have incorporated them to a significant degree in the Latigo y Daga system. Thus, Sayoc kali must be formally credited as being part of the lineage for the Latigo y Daga system.

I am fortunate to have received a duplicate of Momoy's manila rope whip as a gift from Grandmaster Cacoy Canete and have explored various techniques with it for several years. Its action is quite smooth, and it can be effortlessly cracked with great power.

The method of attaching the rope whip to the handle is unique and allows the whip to be spun in a flat vertical plane directly in front of the wielder and to be cracked in that plane as well. The handle of the whip can be easily detached from the whip during use and used as a striking weapon with the whip. This whip is quite versatile and can execute a range of techniques not available with a traditional stock whip or bullwhip. Any training curriculum in the Filipino whip arts would benefit greatly from an exploration of the range of techniques made possible by the unique design of the traditional rope whip.

Part Three

THEORY AND APPLICATIONS

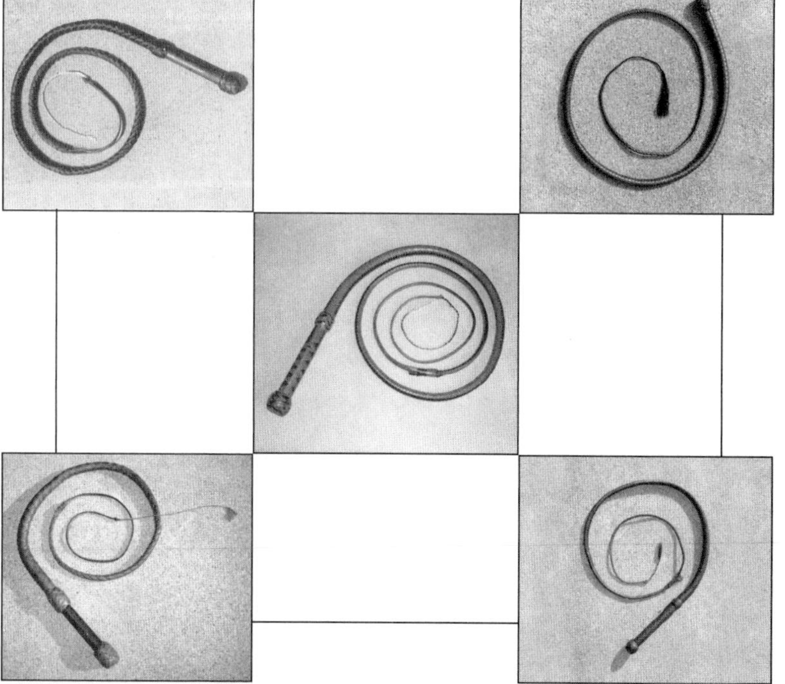

12 Combative Strategy

"The difference between theory and application is that in theory there is no difference."

Now that you have established a foundation in the long-range techniques of Latigo y Daga, it is time to look at medium- and close-range techniques and their theory and application. Combative theory in the Filipino martial arts hinges on the ability to control the fighting range. Stick work is traditionally divided into three ranges: *largo mano, medio,* and *corto* (long, medium, and close).

Some Filipino systems devote themselves exclusively to one of these ranges. The theory behind this is that a high level of proficiency in one range is better than mediocre skills in two or three ranges. But this theory does not necessarily always hold true in actual confrontations.

Even though a particular system may claim to be a long-range style (e.g., the Largo Mano system) or a close-range style (e.g., Angel Cabales' Serrada system), practitioners of these styles also study and practice techniques in other ranges. This is because any experienced practitioner of the combative arts knows that combat

The stick held in long range, where only the hands can be hit.

The stick held in medium range, where the body can be hit and the free hand can come into play to control the opponent's stick.

The stick held in close range, where the free hand can touch the opponent's body. This is also grappling range.

cannot always be controlled and limited to one range and that you must always be ready to deal with the unexpected.

Guro Inosanto often categorizes martial arts into those that are complete arts and those that aren't. This can be viewed from many perspectives. Complete can mean that the system has a full range of techniques for the weaponry used, or it can mean that the arts have techniques that can be used effectively in any range.

If you look at Inosanto-LaCoste Kali, it can be viewed as a complete art in that it has a very full range of weaponry and also encompasses techniques for those weapons that can be used in all ranges. The same applies to Grandmaster Canete's Corto system. Although by its very title it is a close-range system, it includes long-range techniques, medium-range techniques, and a very healthy dose of standing and ground-grappling techniques.

Grandmaster Cacoy began his own pursuit of grappling training 68 years ago at the age of 14 and also actively pursued a study of judo in the 1950s. Aspects of both these styles are actively present in the material he teaches today and are reflected in Latigo y Daga whip grappling techniques.

To properly understand and integrate all these concepts of range control as they apply to the whip, one must have a solid foundation in eskrima, an extended exposure to the whip, and a hands-on knowledge of practical combat. Guro Jeff Finder is thoroughly experienced in all these areas and is ideally qualified to present short-whip combative theory. He was a personal student of Angel Cabales, who awarded him an advanced instructor's certificate. Guro Finder has used a whip for more than 20 years and was a successful member of the 1989 U.S. full-contact eskrima team sent to the Philippines. The following are Guro Finder's observations on the subject of using the short whip.

SHORT-WHIP COMBATIVE THEORY FROM THE SERRADA PERSPECTIVE

Although the Filipino martial art of Serrada escrima is best known for its use of shorter sticks, generally 18 to 24 inches in length, it is rooted firmly in concepts of movement and strategy that lend themselves to use of the short whip, in particular bullwhips up to 6 feet in length.

A characteristic of the Filipino arts in general is constant flowing movement. Serrada uses the short stick to intensively fill a space with density of motion, which is exactly what one would do combatively with the short whip. Since the shorter stick moves more quickly in a smaller space than a longer stick, the short whip is faster and tighter but does sacrifice range. Similarly, because the range is closer, the opponent will also be nearer, and so the rapidness of combat and the need for reflexive speed are greater.

Inertia is a factor that must be overcome, as the time required to physically accelerate can leave one vulnerable when there is little margin for error. Hence, the strategy in close quarters is to maintain speed so that there is little hesitation in reacting to an opponent. You must harness speed efficiently, however, or it opens gaps or leaves you out of position. This is where controlled patterns of motion must coincide with responsive positioning relative to the opponent's movement. The key elements are footwork and body positioning, control of the primary weapon, and use of the free hand or secondary weapon. In this case, your primary weapon is the short whip, and the live hand might carry a knife.

The Latigo y Daga concept recognizes that (1) a skilled and determined opponent might be able to crash the inside range by either timing the whip or entangling it, and (2) the knife is an effective deterrent to such a strategy. A cornerstone concept in Serrada is the ability to hold your ground. The idea is that you might not have the option to move much, such as in a confined space, and that knowing how to maximize your positioning with minimal movement enables you to control the point of impact. An implied supposition is that in such an engagement, you will be able to face the opponent, so the primary footwork, called the *papeet,* is designed to accomplish this.

Sometimes referred to as a "replacement step," the papeet is based on the forward triangle. The lead foot points toward the opponent's centerline, and the rear foot provides the base. You orient toward left- or right-side attacks by establishing right- or left-foot leads, respectively, allowing a natural body alignment toward the direction of incoming energy. As the attack shifts, you can either rotate the point of the triangle or switch feet at the forward point of the triangle to reorient your facing direction; though you face forward, you have a left- or right-side lead and bias.

Since training in Serrada emphasizes holding your ground, and because the weapon is rigid, control of the short stick can be somewhat linear. Much of this does, in fact, translate well to the short whip. Holding your ground is not static; in actuality, it uses a lot of small steps to make finer adjustments rather than bigger steps that cover distance.

Being longer and more flexible, the whip cannot deliver short, chopping blows while in standard use. Like the stick, the whip combines a variety of both linear and circular movements. The essential character of the whip is the speed of its tip. As such, its primary application is at the full range of its motion. This, however, can be modified by use of both foot- and handwork. For example, a full-arm throw of a 4-foot whip, with your weight forward, can reach forward 8 feet because of the extension of the arm and the length of the fall at the end of the whip. However, a short-arm throw, while you shift your weight rearward, can pop the same whip 3 feet or less in front of your own face, certainly close enough to command attention!

As stated earlier, the key to the whip is overcoming inertia through constant motion. I played with whips for perhaps 20 years before discovering this key. Part of the problem was that I had long whips, 8 to 12 feet, which are difficult to keep in motion. I was pretty much stuck on practicing linear cracking moves. Once I got a good short whip, a 4-foot snake, and then realized how energetic its movement could be, practicing came alive for me. Tight, upward, figure eight movement resembles the thrashing of the real snakes I used to catch as a kid, and the better I got with this pattern, the more extension away from me I could manifest with the whip.

Therein lies a significant difference between flowing in defensive holding patterns with the whip and more standard Serrada patterns. Whereas the stick primarily uses downward-angled figure eights and stroking to beat down an opponent, with a whip you want to keep it up off the ground. After all, dragging a whip slows it down, to say nothing of getting dirt into the braiding, which can weaken it or affect flexibility. The upward-stroke figure eight keeps the weapon off the ground and in front of you.

Depending on the width of movement and the energy imparted, the whip can move to cover you side to side, in front parallel to the body, or even extend outward, almost like fencing with a foil. It does take much more skill and energy to achieve, let alone sustain, the last action.

The purpose of the figure eight is not so much for striking as setting up strikes. From this constant circular motion, you can learn to throw a variety of strikes. These can be overhead circular strikes, linear vertical or diagonal throws, reversing cracks, short vertical snaps, etc. Letting the whip become the teacher, you learn to use footwork and body mechanics to place the tip of the whip where you want, essentially creating a dance with the whip as both a partner and an extension of your own energy. More than any other weapon, the whip follows and reveals precisely what energy is fed into its motion.

Fluidity is paramount, and the whip seemingly has a mind of its own. Becoming aware of and using this energy, you fill space with motion, not just in front but in any direction you choose. Though the dance can appear delicate and refined, any misstep reveals the latent power in that movement. The whip can be punishing, not just at the tip but anywhere that coiling energy is unleashed.

As you move in harmony with the whip, the free hand plays a significant role. First, the arm helps to balance the weight and extension of the whip. Second, and this is very important, the hand is there to deflect, block, or otherwise intercept the whip should it come back in toward you.

In mythology, real snakes have no compassion, biting those who try to befriend them. The analogy of the snake is appropriate, as a whip can do the same. You should first learn basic lines of motion to avoid dangerous mistakes before going into more integrated movement. However, if you're like me, the integrated full-body movement enabled me to make sense of my simple moves. Just remember that any body part hit by the whip can be hurt and that the face is especially vulnerable.

Such flowing arts as eskrima, arnis, and tai chi are well suited to incorporating the movement of the whip. These are energetically sensitive arts, so the concept of extending your energy using patterns of motion and flow is not foreign, but rather can be adapted and incorporated into your own expression of your art. Thus, full-body dynamics and interrelated patterns of hand motion from stick, sword, or empty hand can be adapted easily to the whip. Not only is this beautiful and dynamic, it is also a way to explore the dangerous edge that whipping implies.

• • •

Guro Finder's theories on short-whip work are an excellent summary of the Filipino perspective on the whip, and they are the perfect stepping-stone to move from theory to the study of combative application.

13 Range Control Techniques for the Short Whip

With a solid foundation in Latigo y Daga long-range techniques and an understanding of short-whip theory, you must now develop practical skills in moving from long range to medium range. Significantly greater skills are required in the use of the free hand to control the thong of the whip and to keep the whip clear of your body.

MEDIUM-RANGE WHIP WORK

The basic long-range techniques in Latigo y Daga are virtually identical to those in medium range, with the primary difference being the use of footwork to shorten the working range of the whip. As noted in the Latigo y Daga basics section, you throw the first five strikes with the lead leg and the whip in the forward position. This maximizes the effective range of the whip and provides a foundation for walking forward while striking with the whip.

When working in medium range, change the footwork to retracted footwork, which puts the weapon hand to the rear of the leading foot. This simple change alone can effectively reduce the working combative range by as much as 2 feet. With the retraction of the arm toward the rear, you can further reduce the distance by another foot. Moving from a lower knob grip on the whip to one at the upper knob can gain you another foot. The net result of this adjustment is to change the working range of a 6-foot whip from 8 feet to 4 feet away from the

This demonstrates the available range with forward footwork.

body, which places the techniques solidly in the middle range for a short whip.

A proper combination of these elements gives you the option of working at long range or moving into medium range with a simple step and change in body position. The transition from long to medium range can usually be done in the time it takes to initiate a basic slash and pull it through to completion.

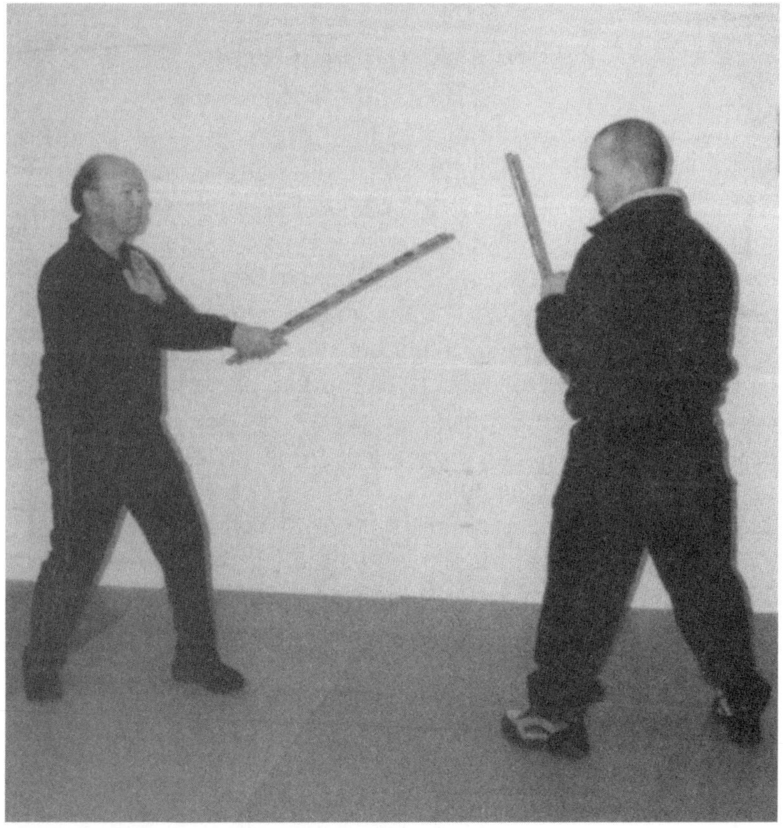

This demonstrates how the range changes with retracted footwork.

The footwork is reversed in synchronization with the slash, and the line continuation of the completed slash positions the whip for the next motion, which is now in medium range. The real-world time for this transition is under a quarter of a second.

These simple techniques allow you to change from long range to middle range and back to long range with no superfluous motions. With practice, you can seamlessly integrate these techniques into a personalized individual flow, which allows you to dynamically control the range of combat at will.

CLOSE-RANGE WHIP WORK

In one respect, close-range whip work is not true whip work at all, but rather is the application of close-range eskrima techniques with the whip folded in half. You can achieve the basic grip for the folded whip by holding the handle of the whip and the knotted end of the thong in the same hand. This creates a loop in the whip and also allows the fall and popper to hang underneath the hand.

A 4-foot whip folded in half becomes a very versatile tool. It can be used as a heavy and powerful flail or an instrument for delivering strong butt strikes. It can also function effectively as a grappling aid using Filipino rope fighting techniques, and the tail end of the whip can still be used to flick an opponent's face or eyes. With the whip in this position, you can apply virtually every basic baton technique, as well as all the strikes, blocks, counters, and disarming techniques of any Filipino system.

To apply these close-range techniques, you must first be able to make the transition from using the whip at its full extension to gripping it in the folded position. You can easily develop the skills for this transition by using a very simple technique.

The first part of this technique is to throw a forehand, horizontal number-three slash from the Latigo y Daga system. Allow the whip to wrap around your waist on the left side and then capture it against the left hip with the left hand in the palm-inward position. With the knot of the thong trapped in the left hand, bring it over to the right hand, which opens and

---

The following photos show the transition to the folded-whip position for the application of close-range eskrima techniques.

Throw the whip on the number-three line.

Capture the whip against the left hip.

The left hand brings the thong forward to meet the right hand.

The left hand places the thong into the right hand.

The whip is now in the folded, or half-whip, position.

captures the knot of the thong next to the handle of the whip. The whip is now in the folded position and fully gripped in the right hand.

This technique is easy to practice, and you can become proficient in a short time. Once you have mastered the technique for the transition to the folded-whip position, you can integrate this manipulation skill into the normal flow of other whip techniques. Further practice allows you to execute this technique with a knife held in your left hand.

With extended practice, you can transition to the folded-whip position in less than a third of a second. Being able to execute this technique at this speed is essential to combat survival, particularly when an opponent has decided not to deal with the whip in long range and chooses to crash directly to close range.

One of the great strengths of the folded-whip transition is the ability to change the whip instantly from a close-range weapon to a medium- or long-range weapon. You accomplish this simply by relaxing the grip on the thong of the whip when you throw the whip. The thong will extend outward as the whip unfolds, and the range of the weapon changes from close range all the way out to long range as quickly as the whip can extend itself.

It is essential to develop strong working skills that enable you to change seamlessly from one range to another and back again. The ability to be comfortable in any range of combat is necessary to survival and is an indication of the level of your mastery of the whip. The techniques presented here provide a means to technically explore short-whip theory in all three combat ranges. The last stage in this exploration is to study the dynamics of these techniques in actual sparring.

Sparring with the Whip

Sparring is one of the most dangerous phases of the study of the whip. Sparring is a form of controlled fighting that balances on that fine line between engaging in actual combat and maintaining the safety of the participants.

Ideally, sparring is a learning vehicle for both parties, and the rules of engagement govern the degree of learning. In some types of sparring, one player will allow the other to gain the upper hand as part of the learning process. At the other extreme, the "friendly" sparring match degenerates into a good, solid brawl. In both situations, learning occurs, but what is actually learned from each experience is quite different.

Safe sparring with the whip requires both participants to have significant fighting skills, a high level of personal self-control, tight control of the emotional aspects of combat, and the ability to instantly break off the engagement at the first sign of true danger.

This photo demonstrates the validity of one of the Dog Brothers' maxims: "When the rules do not specifically prohibit it, grappling happens."

These qualities are the hallmark of the Dog Brothers. As explained previously, the Dog Brothers' system was created to explore full-contact weapons fighting at its most unrestricted level. At the time of the Dog Brothers' inception, 1989, a typical Filipino martial arts tournament involved heavily padding either the weapons or the participants. In either case, the striking power of the weapons was so diminished that most fighters simply waded in and ignored being struck. In addition, it became impossible to establish the validity of any given technique since the power of the strikes was so nullified.

The Dog Brothers' response to this was to collect a group of fighters willing to engage with a bare minimum of body armor to create a more valid forum for exploring Filipino stick fighting. Their first meeting in a public park was highly successful and set the tone for what is now the world standard by which full-contact weapon fighting is judged. Dog Brothers fighters have only two rules: "No suing for nothing, no how, no way," and, more importantly, "Be friends at the end of the day."

The Dog Brothers group now has a cadre of instructors in the system, a large international membership, and a curriculum that offers sparring matches for virtually any weapon the participant desires. So far, these matches have included fights with the staff, the bokken, the nunchaku, the three sectional staff, wooden knives, the Tapado stick, and the whip. Light fencing masks and batting gloves have replaced the original armor of heavy traditional eskrima headgear and hockey gloves for some participants.

I was fortunate to begin sparring with the Dog Brothers in 1990, which ultimately led to the whip sparring matches with Eric Knaus documented in the Dog Brothers video series. To some degree, these sparring matches have become legendary, mostly because they were the first of their kind and have yet to be attempted by anyone else since.

Fortunately, a video record of the matches exists, but watching the videos can provide only one perspective on the sparring matches. The other perspective must come from the participants. With this in mind, I recently interviewed Eric to obtain his recollection of the events. These are his thoughts.

> Initially Marc Denny tried to talk me out of fighting against the whip. He had seen Tom cutting individual leaves off a tree with his whip, and he felt it would be wiser to err on the side of safety. I was very intrigued by the thought of trying to fight a really cool kind of exotic weapon, one with a tip that could cut like a knife. I thought of the whip as a long-range knife, a sort of "flying knife." My strategy was to think of timing it like a jump rope. That was the only analogy I could think of.
>
> My understanding of long whips was that they were designed to work effectively off horseback. This extra length would be a drawback on the ground and would make fighting a 10-foot whip easier because it takes longer to create an orbit around its user, and it would be easier to time the entry.
>
> At the time, I chose not to wear any hand protection because I thought if Tom could hit my hands, he would have to be pretty good. I used the experience as a study in closing techniques. With the long whip, I could feel the power of the whip's pop when the air hit my chest or face. My internalization of this whole process was that it was like trying to learn the mechanics of the fight as on-the-job training.
>
> The short whip was very different. The first barrage of strikes kept me on my heels due to its shorter recoil time. I lost that sliver of time between the strikes. With the short whip, there was a much smaller fraction of time available to close if I wanted to press it.
>
> I saw this as a two-way learning process: Tom can't grow unless I push him, and the consequence of that

> strategy is that I might have to take a whip shot. He might cut me up, but if he doesn't drop me, I have a chance. As far as doing it again, I see that there is a strong likelihood of getting cut by the whip. Once you draw blood, though, there is a price to pay. Then you have to ask yourself where you draw the line for training and ask yourself what you are trying to accomplish. I enjoyed the process.
>
> During my "ronin" years, I learned that if you talk the talk, you have to walk the walk. Although Marc was apprehensive at the time, I was more than willing and looked forward to doing it. As a result I am a better person for it and broke ground that hasn't been broken in centuries and that no one else in Dog Brothers has wanted to do since.

Eric is called the "Top Dog" in the Dog Brothers group for good reason. Those who have sparred with him realize very quickly that he is an extremely competent fighter and a skilled technician. He is an excellent technical analyst and can clearly articulate the strengths and weaknesses of both players in a postfight analysis.

It was for these reasons that I agreed to the whip sparring matches with Eric. I had sparred with Eric and other Dog Brothers on quite a few occasions with training knives and sticks, and the intensity of the learning from these experiences was considerable. These experiences had sparked an interest in doing some actual whip sparring, but I had been unable to find anyone willing to explore this totally new territory. By this time, Eric had fought against players with the bokken, nunchaku, and everything else, including small tree limbs. His willingness to fight against unusual weapons was unique, and this, combined with his technical skill level, made him an ideal partner for something that posed clear dangers to both participants.

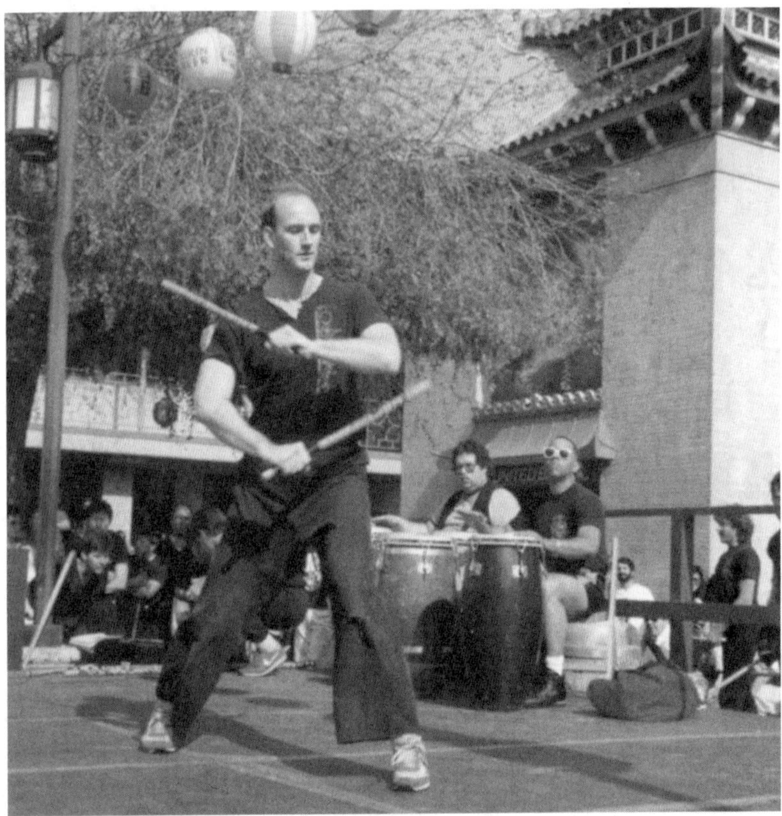

Eric Knaus demonstrates his double-stick technique.

As the whip fighter, I could wear no hand protection because protective gloves would seriously hinder proper manipulation of the whip. Eric has a well-earned reputation as someone who can close the distance and do so while maintaining tremendous striking power. If he did succeed in closing, my hands would be the primary target during his entry and would be totally unprotected.

The risks to Eric were totally unknown in actual sparring. The main targets for combative whip work are the eyes, face, throat, groin, and hands, in that order. The face mask should, in theory, protect the face and eyes and provide limited protection for the throat. It would not, however, protect the eyes from small sticks or rocks that the whip can often unintentionally launch at tremendous speed. Any whip also has the ability to easily rupture the windpipe, which normally results in death.

Eric's choice to not wear hand gear increased the risks of lacerations and broken bones, which are the normal risks for Dog Brothers' sparring. Eric's questions of "where do you draw the line for training, and what are you trying to accomplish?" were not rhetorical, but topics we discussed in detail both before and after sparring.

My recollection is that our goals were to (1) demonstrate that whip sparring was actually feasible, (2) determine the viability of the stick against the whip, (3) evaluate the difficulty of closing on both the long and the short whip, and (4) determine what happens to the whip fighter once the range is closed or greatly diminished.

Eric and I had conflicting areas of self-confidence: he truly did not believe that I could hit his hands, and I was quite convinced that I could pick off individual fingers if I chose to. I was genuinely concerned that I might accidentally hit his throat or have the lash go through the bars of the helmet, and did not see these as safety risks that could be counterbalanced by the "learning experience."

We agreed that we would stay off each other's hands since we were both unarmored and that we would exercise caution in the early stages of the play until we both had the feel of things. I resolved to use the sparring as an exercise in range control and felt I could do this by cracking the whip a safe distance from his face and body, and thus allow the crack to do the actual work for me. Ultimately I was cracking 12 to 18 inches from his face and body, and immediately afterward he expressed surprise at the power of the explosions going off in his face.

These fights are documented on tape number six of the Dog Brothers video series, and they make an excellent study of the stick against other weapons and the whip in particular. A careful analysis of Eric's closing techniques shows the whip cracking directly in front of his face and his beginning his charge just as the end of the whip continues on by. This shows both the timing and courage necessary to close on a whip. Eric did, in fact, prove quite thoroughly that a good man with a stick can close and tackle a man with a whip, and do it more than once.

Eric commented later that if I held a knife in my free hand, I would have a better chance against someone crashing into close range. This sparring experience, and that single comment, ultimately became the springboard for the development of many of the techniques of the Latigo y Daga system as it is today.

There are many ways to explore whip sparring, and they all have some degree of risk. No one should ever consider whip sparring until he has refined his techniques and target work to the degree of pinpoint accuracy. This is the only way to provide any margin of safety for the players involved and to ensure that safety concerns are not compromised in the pursuit of learning.

Maestro Snookie Sanchez and His Metaphysical Approach to the Whip of Kali Intra

"When I do these demonstrations I jeopardize my art, my teaching, and my students, but I do it because I have mastered the whip!"

—Snookie Sanchez

No treatise on the subject of the Filipino whip arts would be complete without an examination of the applications perfected by Maestro Sanchez. Born in 1938, Eustaquio "Snookie" Sanchez II was one of the foremost practitioners of the Filipino whip arts. His practical skills and the full life he led made him a legend in the kali community.

One of Snookie's trademarks was physical toughness, which he developed early on as a frogman in the U.S. Coast Guard. His specialty was detonating mines out at sea. During the Korean War, he would place the explosives on the mines and then swim back to the Coast Guard pickup boat. If he missed his pickup, he would have to keep swimming until he was out of the range of the explosion. Once after one of his pickups, he was thrown from the Coast Guard boat during a storm and had to survive several days at sea before being rescued. When he was finally pulled from the water, his skin had turned a bluish-purple color. Recuperating in the hospital after this ordeal, Snookie exercised by lifting his bed and running laps late at night.

Following his recovery, Snookie realized that he really had something special: a strong inner power and a feeling of invincibility. It was at this point that he began his kali training under Grandmaster Ben Largusa. He trained with Grandmaster Largusa for 5 years in the San Francisco area and later returned to Hawaii to found his own style of kali called Kali Intra, or "inside fighting." He named his school the Universal Fighting Star and took the kali concepts of universality and applied them to all aspects of his martial art—the whip, the stick, and the knife.

Once he was back in Hawaii, Snookie found that he was being regularly challenged because of his reputation. This meant the he often had to apply his skills as a kali man both in his day-to-day life and at the liquor store and gas station where he was employed. On one occasion a man approached Snookie at his bank and asked, "Are you Snookie Sanchez?" As soon as Snookie confirmed that he was, the man attacked him with a pair of nunchaku. Snookie waited for the appropriate moment, snaked the nunchaku out of the man's hand, and disarmed him. He kept the nunchucks in a box along with the knives and other weapons he had taken from people who challenged him.

Snookie kept himself in top physical and mental condition and on more than one occasion allowed people to drive cars over his stomach. Photos and videos taken of Snookie during this era attest to his exceptional level of physical conditioning. Maestro Snookie's feats cannot be attributed to simple physical training alone, however. Snookie had developed the power of *anting-anting,* a branch of the Filipino mystical arts. Dismissed by many as superstition, the power of anting-anting is very real to those who have observed it firsthand, including me. Contemporaries of Snookie described him like this: "He had some kind of aura, something mystical about him. He could stare right through you and melt you, literally destroy you with his eyes."

It was Snookie's ability with the whip, however, that really made him stand out among other martial artists. Snookie had trained with the latigo whip as a youth and always included it in his arsenal of kali weapons. During the late 1970s, a promoter organized a tournament that would allow the competitors to choose any weapon they desired. Players from all styles, including kendo and eskrima, signed up. When Snookie filled out his entry form, he listed the 10-foot bullwhip as his weapon of choice.

A rumor circulated that a "group of Moro fighters from the Philippines" were coming over to fight in the tournament, and this so intimidated the other contestants that they all backed out. Maestro Snookie, after downing a shot of tequila to calm his nerves, showed up at the tournament ready to fight all comers, only to find out that the Moros, hearing of his reputation with the whip, had backed out as well. Snookie thus found himself the only contestant standing in the arena.

Snookie's skill at putting out candles with his whip while he was blindfolded was what ultimately elevated him far above the rest. Snookie demonstrated this skill regularly and even allowed it to be videotaped on numerous occasions. He would lay out a ring of candles around him, have a spectator blindfold him, and then put out the candles with his whip. He would also have his students kneel in front of him with candles set on the brims of their baseball caps. Again he would be blindfolded and then put the candles out. He clearly represented this skill as metaphysical, and it is interesting to see how the concentration involved in these demonstrations took so much energy out of him.

Maestro Snookie attributed these powers to early training he had as a youth. Sanchez was orphaned at an early age and raised in the sugar plantations in Kahuku, Hawaii. He spent a portion of his youth in the company of the local village shaman. This priestess developed a lot of affection for the young boy, and she gave him an *orascion*, one of the three Latin books of prayers she had. Snookie kept the book all his life. The orascion is a very personal thing and is traditionally used in prayer by Filipino fighters to make them invincible. Some eskrimadors have their orascion tattooed on their bodies, and it can be a powerful tool for meditation for them. Most orascions are in Latin, but some of the older eskrimadors believe the prayers must be in Hebrew to develop real power.

The priestess who gave Snookie his orascion had the ability to sense light. Maestro Snookie used to describe how she could point to a candle and manipulate the way it flickered. He said the whole room would shake as she recited her prayers. Maestro Snookie practiced the skills this priestess taught him and developed the ability to sense light from candles through a blindfold. He combined this talent with his whip work, and what resulted were the demonstrations that made him famous.

Some people dismiss this sort of demonstration as some form of magic trick because of the blindfold. These people are missing a fundamental point: it takes a very high skill level to put out candles even when you can clearly see the target. Most Western whip artists put out candles through physical contact, that is, with the whip lying across the flame. This allows for a great margin of error because they can use any part of the last foot or so of the whip to put out the flame. Maestro Snookie always used the air from the actual pop of the whip or just the very tip of the popper to put out the candles.

I have reviewed videotapes of four different demonstrations by Maestro Snookie and his students, and there are several things that stand out in detail. The first is that Maestro Snookie demonstrated a remarkable degree of physical conditioning. Second, he clearly was very highly skilled in the art of kali, which his students demonstrated as well. Third, his skill and accuracy with the whip were comparable to those of any of the professional Western whip artists. He reinforced his accuracy with the whip when he won a bet he made with some Mexican cowboys that he could pop the tail off a scorpion that was walking by.

The following photos show a blindfolded Maestro Snookie extinguishing the flames of candles being held by his assistants. These photos were captured as still images from extremely rare video footage of the maestro demonstrating his unique skill.

Blindfolded and kneeling, Maestro Snookie prepares himself to put out the candles.

He draws the whip back.

The whip comes forward and puts out the first candle.

After this demonstration, the cowboys gave him the nickname "El Alacran," which means "the Scorpion" in Spanish.

Maestro Snookie's demonstrations always included putting out candles both with and without the blindfold, and his accuracy didn't degrade when he was blindfolded. In both cases, in the videos you can see that when he missed with the whip it was by fractions of an inch. The flame of the candle visibly moved in response to the air movement created by the pop of the whip. When he finally did put the flame out, more often than not, there was no contact with the whip to the candle.

The photos shown in this chapter are stills taken from a video done by Michael Janich at the University of Hawaii on July 7, 1994, during one of Maestro Snookie's demonstrations. In the photos, you can see that the blindfold he used covered not only his eyes but practically his whole face.

Guro Jeff Finder reviewed a similar video that was done at the Braulio Pedoy Eskrima school on July 28, 1991, and observed: "I was originally shown this Snookie Sanchez video by my friend Dan Medina. Medina commented that he had personally inspected the blindfold used in the demonstration and stated that it was a genuine blindfold."

Guro Finder has extensive training in the Chinese martial arts and noted that Maestro Snookie always extended his left hand palm outward from his body during his blindfolded whip work. Guro Finder commented that this was very consistent with the Chinese philosophy that the left hand senses and receives energy and the right hand delivers it.

In my opinion, the best way to approach these demonstrations is with the same philosophy used by Sherlock Holmes: "When you have eliminated the impossible, whatever remains, however improbable, must be the truth." Clearly, the skill level demonstrated by Maestro Snookie with his whip was far beyond the norm, and his own explanation of his skills, however improbable, is most likely the truth.

Maestro Snookie shows the tremendous physical condition that he maintained all his life.

Snookie Sanchez was an artist, a woodcarver, a humanitarian, a friend to his students, and a master of the whip. He died of natural causes in 1996 and will always be remembered for the legacy he left behind. Maestro Snookie was known by many names, but for those who knew him well, he will always be remembered by the name he worked hardest for, because he was truly Snookie "King of the Whip" Sanchez.

An Overview of Advanced Material for the Short Whip

The whip is one of the most versatile weapons to study, and there are numerous areas for developing advanced techniques. Some of these areas have direct combative applications, whereas others develop pure manipulation skills. However, all of them have value, and as you explore and play with them, you will find those that suit your style, which you can then develop into an area of specialty.

TARGET WORK

Target work is probably the most important area of study for the combative whip stylist. The best techniques in the world are useless unless they can help you place the whip on target. A favorite trick for mule skinners was to pop flies off a mule's ear without hitting the ear itself. This kind of skill came from endless practice during the empty hours of a long trip, which could sometimes last for weeks or even months.

The key here is practice, and this is reflected by the many contemporary Western whip artists who can, among their standard tricks, duplicate this accuracy by cutting a piece of newspaper into tiny pieces, severing cigarettes out of a partner's mouth, and picking handkerchiefs from a pocket. They can also fire a handgun hanging from a string, pull weapons out of someone's hand, and drive tacks into a board. Vince Bruce can cut a cigarette out of his own mouth and can cut cards in half as he throws them in the air in rapid succession.

There are many ways to improvise targets with which to practice, including placing soda cans on a fence, taping spaghetti to a wall, or resting matchsticks on a table. The whip makes an excellent garden and yard maintenance tool, and every tree has individual leaves that can be picked off with the whip. Candles are considered among the most difficult targets, particularly if just the air movement from the pop of the whip is used to put them out.

Guro Sonny Umpad uses several Filipino variants on target practice in his whip training. He likes to take the handle from an old spoon, sharpen one end, and attach it to the popper of a whip. He then practices throwing the whip and trying to stick the spoon handle into a target marked on a board. He also hangs a loop of iron from a string and practices throwing the tip of the whip through the ring.

WRAPPING AND LOCKING

The whip can be locked onto almost any object, including chair and table legs, fence rails, and weapons held in someone's hand. Wrapping is fairly easy, but locking is a difficult and subtle process of tying a free running knot with the whip on the given target. The knot prevents the object from being released by

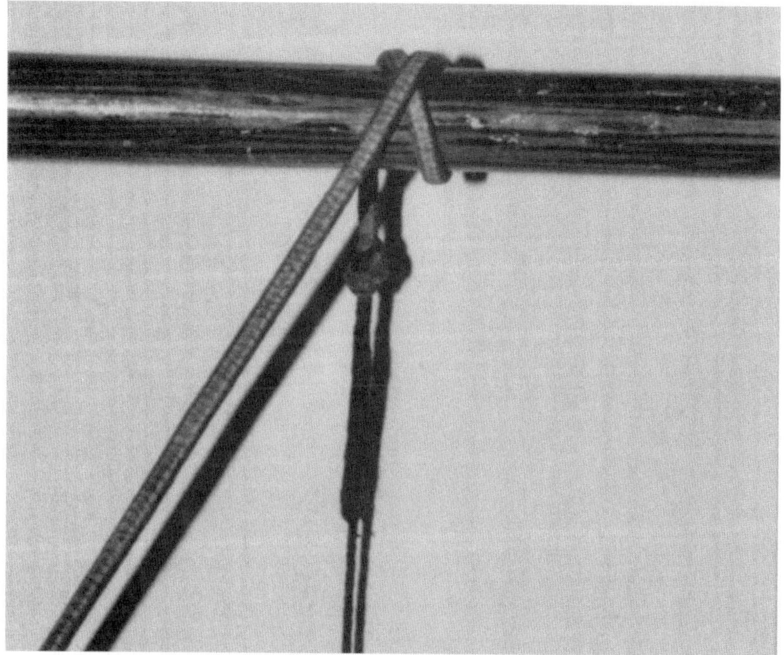

The fall of a whip locked in place with a free running knot.

the whip, but the knot itself can be undone with a simple movement to relax the end of the whip. Wrapping and locking require enough precision to place the fall knot at a precise place on the target. Generally, the fall knot should be just on the target or just behind it for successful wrapping and locking.

CLOCK DRILLS

Clock drills can be done by visualizing a clock in front of you or at each of your sides. Each of the hours on the clock can be used as a target, and the imaginary clocks at each side can also be used as a gauge of where to begin and end strikes. A clock can be drawn in chalk on the ground and strikes can be thrown at 3:00, 6:00, and 9:00 o'clock or at any other hour.

If you have a clock sketched on the ground around you and strike 11:00, 7:00, 1:00, and 5:00 o'clock in that order, you will have done a four-corners drill. It is easiest to begin this drill without trying to crack the whip and then to add the cracks once the gross motions are developed. The four-corners drill provides a foundation for dealing with multiple attackers from all angles. Clock drills can be done using all backhands, all forehands, or any other desired combination of movements.

The clock face as it is visualized on the ground.

OLISI-TOYUK DRILLS

The olisi-toyuk is the Filipino variant of the rice flail and has a complete training regimen all its own. The primary techniques for this weapon involve extensive twirling, catching, and striking with the weapon. These motions are identical to those used combatively with a short whip.

The Okinawan, Japanese, and Chinese arts all have a wide array of technical material that applies to the rice flail, or nunchaku. There is an extensive amount of printed and video material on the nunchaku, and these materials are an excellent resource for developing advanced manipulation skills with the short whip.

PARTNER DRILLS

You can do partner drills by facing a partner and feeding attacks to each other from a safe distance. This allows you to see how the whip looks when it is thrown at you, and you can also use your whip to try to catch or lock the tip of the opponent's whip.

FILIPINO FORMS

Virtually all Filipino systems have traditional exhibition forms, also known as *sayaw* or *pormas,* and several of these styles have forms adapted specifically for whip use. In general, any form for the stick, stick and dagger, or sword and dagger can be readily used for the whip or whip and dagger. Forms training can include using the knife in the point-up and point-down positions or gripping the stick in the normal and inverted positions.

Carrenza is the Filipino term for creative forms that are made up as you flow from one technique to the next. Done properly, they have many dancelike aspects. Carrenza training is an excellent way to develop visualization skills, flow, and graceful movement.

HAND SWITCHING

One of the most difficult skills to develop with a whip is proficiency with both hands. The best whip artists are equally capable with their left or right hand. Training the nondominant hand can be as time consuming as, or more so than, the original training with the dominant hand.

The best way to begin hand switching is to practice a technique with one hand half a dozen times and then try the same technique with the other hand half a dozen times. Then try the technique switching the whip back and forth between hands until you are proficient.

You will be developing new muscles in your nondominant arm, and the techniques may begin to deteriorate as these muscles tire. At this point, let the arm rest and resume the training the next day. Ambidextrous drills will greatly improve your free-hand skills and are an essential base to have for exploring multiple-whip techniques.

MULTIPLE WHIPS

The Filipino martial arts have double-stick *sinawali* (weaving) drills. These drills teach symmetrical and asymmetrical movement with a stick in each hand and are ideal for double-whip training. There are easily 20 or 30 basic sinawali patterns in each system, and any experienced Filipino martial arts instructor can quickly teach you the basics of this portion of the arts.

Anthony DeLongis demonstrates the use of matched long whips.

Multiple-whip work begins with a foundation in hand switching and then progresses to using one matched whip in each hand, or a long whip in one hand and a short whip in the other, two or three whips in one hand, and long and short whips in one hand.

The matched-whip drills are identical to the basic sinawali drills, but when you move to using unmatched whip lengths, the timing changes considerably. With multiple matched whips in one hand, you get two or three simultaneous cracks. If you use multiple short whips in one hand, the techniques for cracking the whip are no different from those used for a single whip. If you use a long and short whip in one hand, you can get two cracks slightly delayed from each other with a single throw.

KNEELING DRILLS AND GROUNDWORK

The whip can be effectively used from both the kneeling and lying positions. You can progress from standing to kneeling to lying and back to standing again, just as in traditional Filipino stick drills. Some surprising things can be done with the whip using low-line attacks, including leg and ankle wraps.

GRAPPLING WITH THE WHIP

Grappling with the whip is worthy of a book of its own. Grappling techniques for the whip come from Indonesian sarong techniques, Filipino rope techniques, and Filipino bandanna techniques. Using the whip in the folded position creates a loop that has many powerful grappling applications that cross over into the techniques found in other styles. One of these is the Pananandata style of Grandmaster Amante Marinas Sr. Grandmaster Marinas is an expert with the rope and the latiko whip, and his Pananandata system is a great resource for anyone interested in grappling techniques with flexible weapons.

Another excellent resource is Guro Larry Hartsell, one of the most broad-based grappling instructors and the top Jeet Kune Do grappler in the world. He has extensive training in Inosanto-LaCoste Kali, sarong and bandanna techniques, rope techniques, and virtually every known type of grappling art. His Jeet

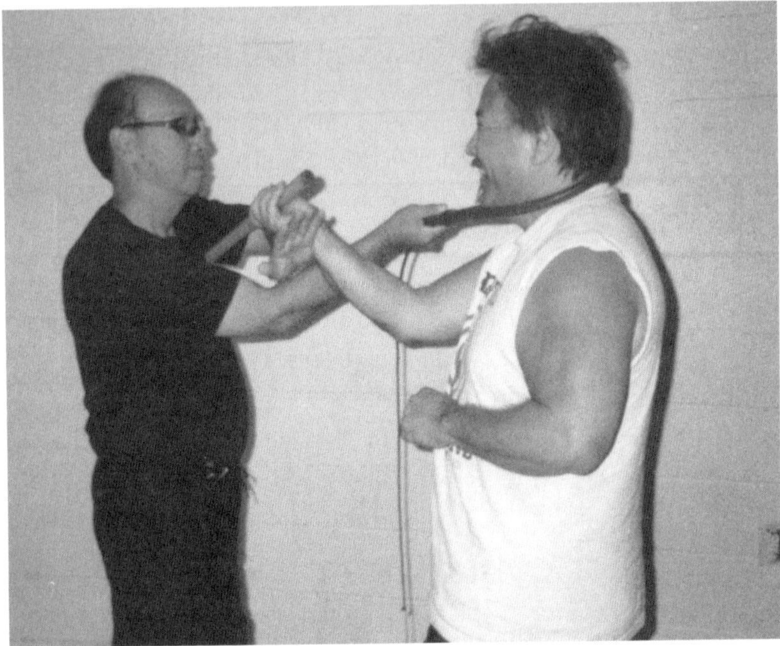

Professor Ron Lew demonstrates the use of the whip as an aid to grappling.

Kune Do grappling association is a complete resource for martial artists interested in flexible-weapons grappling techniques and grappling in general. My first grappling training was under Guro Hartsell, and this book reflects many aspects of his training and philosophy.

Self-Defense with the Whip

During any discussion of whips for self-defense, the subject of improvised whips inevitably comes up. These discussions principally center on using a belt or car antenna as a readily available self-defense tool.

IMPROVISED WHIPS

The belt is in fact a very good weapon, mostly as a flail in middle range and then as an aid to grappling in close range. Inosanto-LaCoste Kali, as well as any other system, has formal belt techniques. From the standpoint of the traditional whip arts, a belt cannot replace a true whip. The real problem with the belt as a weapon is that most people wear it to hold their pants up, and the last thing you really want to be doing during a fight is trying to hit someone with a belt in one hand while you are holding your pants up with the other hand.

The car antenna is considered a classic improvised weapon and certainly has technical applications of its own for self-defense. One problem with using a car antenna is that the amount of effort required to remove it is considerably greater than most people realize. The next problem comes while breaking off the antenna. If it is a straight-wire antenna, it will have a really nasty sharp end that can slice your own hand if your grip slips. An electric antenna, on the other hand, is virtually impossible to break off because of the heavy nylon core joining the sections to the motor. Anyone who doesn't believe this should go to a wrecking yard with a pair of heavy gloves and break off a few electric antennas. You will find that it takes some time to break one, and it will have an even nastier broken end than the solid antenna. Of course, the standard response to this problem with the jagged end is to just switch grips and put the jagged end forward.

The fundamental problem with the whole antenna-as-a-weapon theory is that if you have enough time to find a car, break off its antenna, and switch grips, then your attacker is not physically close enough to be dangerous, and you should really be running away rather than wasting your time improvising weapons.

Marc "Animal" MacYoung, one of the foremost authorities in the area of street self-defense, has this to say about using car antennas as improvised weapons:

> Remember that I am talking about over 25 years ago. Back then the antennas were hollow little rods made of cheap, flimsy metal. We'd rock 'em back and forth a few times to establish a crack at the base and then roll them in a flat, circular motion parallel to the hood to stress the metal enough to break. The whole process would take from 30 seconds to a minute before the metal fatigued enough to break. Even then sometimes it didn't work. It was never a just-grab-and-rip-it-off move.

MacYoung has produced 10 books and five videos on the subject of street self-defense applications, and these are highly recommended to those interested in a detailed study of improvised weapons and other self-defense related issues.

LEGAL STATUS OF THE WHIP

The subject of the legal consequences of using a whip for self-defense is an interesting one. Every state in America has its own laws, and there are always overriding federal statutes.

To the best of my knowledge, there are no states that classify the whip as a weapon in the same category as knives, nunchaku, batons, and the like. The reason for this appears to be fairly straightforward: whips are used universally in all states as a tool of animal husbandry. It is not viewed any differently from a bridle, pitchfork, or any other commonplace tool found on farms or ranches.

I have given numerous training seminars on officer safety to California law enforcement officers. Before these seminars, none of the officers identified the whip as a weapon or felt that seeing one carried on the seat of a car was a personal threat or in violation of any law in the state. After I demonstrated how to deploy a whip through a car window, they changed their opinions on the use of the whip as a weapon but still maintained that it was legal to carry a whip openly.

Australia has laws that border on Draconian at times, and at one point the Latigo y Daga Association came under fire for promoting the use of the knife with a whip, which some felt would antagonize Australian lawmakers and could jeopardize the outback cowboys' right to carry their whips.

Apparently no such laws have been passed, but it does demonstrate the fact that focusing attention on a particular weapon and its self-defense or combative uses can bring unwelcome attention from lawmakers.

The whip is enjoying a noticeable increase in popularity in the martial arts, and it is safe to assume that at some point in the next 10 years, government agencies will enact laws regarding its carry and use.

Because of repercussions from the September 11, 2001, terrorist attacks in the United States, the bullwhip now clearly appears on the list of forbidden carry-on items posted in every U.S. airport. This is quite a change from when I would routinely carry a bag of whips, wooden daggers, and related supplies onto the plane.

The best recommendation for understanding the legal ramifications of using the whip for self-defense is to study the laws of your own state and country, and then have them explained to you by your local district attorney or judge.

18 The Future of the Whip in the Filipino Martial Arts

Traditionally, the origin of the Filipino martial arts is traced back to A.D. 1521, when Rajah LapuLapu killed Ferdinand Magellan as the Portuguese explorer (sailing for the king of Spain) invaded Mactan Island. During their occupation of the Philippines, the Spaniards destroyed the majority of Filipino written history, including records of its martial arts. The information that we have today on pre-1900 Filipino martial arts was preserved and passed on within the native dance forms.

In 1898 it became legal in the Philippines to publicly practice the martial arts, and thus the first generation of contemporary Filipino martial artists matured. The founding in 1932 of the Cebu Doce Pares Society can be seen as a symbol of this maturity and the beginning of the formal documentation of the Filipino martial arts that we have today. The Filipinos are highly literate, and this process of teaching and documenting their native martial arts was carried on throughout the archipelago.

World War II claimed the lives of many of the Philippines' best fighters and eskrimadors, men who sacrificed themselves to defend their homeland. The Japanese killed the Saavedras brothers and hundreds more like them, both in battle and in prisoner-of-war camps. Their arts, however, were successfully passed on to what became the postwar generation of eskrimadors, who then began disseminating these arts throughout the world.

The number of non-Filipino eskrimadors was very small in the 1950s, and it wasn't until 1966 when Angel Cabales opened the first public Filipino martial arts academy in Stockton, California, that the popularity of eskrima began to truly blossom worldwide. One of Cabales' students, a young man named Dan Inosanto, has spent a lifetime exploring the Filipino martial arts and founded what has become one of the largest worldwide organizations of Filipino martial artists currently in existence.

Almost 40 years later, the legacy established by Angel Cabales, Dan Inosanto, the Canete family, and many more like them has turned the Filipino martial arts into one of the most popular and thriving fighting arts in the world today. This popularity has created a near insatiable thirst for information on techniques of the Filipino arts, and this is reflected in the proliferation of books and videos now available on the topic.

In 1987, when I began researching this book, the written documentation on whip techniques in the Filipino martial arts consisted of just two pages of technical information. Seven years later, because of the efforts of the Latigo y Daga Association, these two pages of information had been expanded enough to create a small pamphlet on the subject. Since that time, with support from such eskrima groups as the Inosanto Instructors Association and the Sayoc clan, rising interest in the whip and dagger arts has resulted in a wealth of newly documented whip techniques and the beginnings of technical exchange among the various styles. Because of this renewed interest, there are now more than 25 documented and certified whip instructors in the different styles of the Filipino martial arts.

With the publication of this text, an entirely new platform exists to support whip practitioners as they continue their own process of uncovery. Their discoveries, added to those of the countless generations of eskrimadors before them, will continue the legacy and evolution of the gift that is the Filipino martial arts.

Part Four

Resources for Practitioners of the Whip Arts

The resources listed here will be of aid to anyone interested in the Filipino martial arts, particularly the whip and dagger arts. All the individuals and organizations are established leaders in their respective fields and are highly recommended for training and technical assistance.

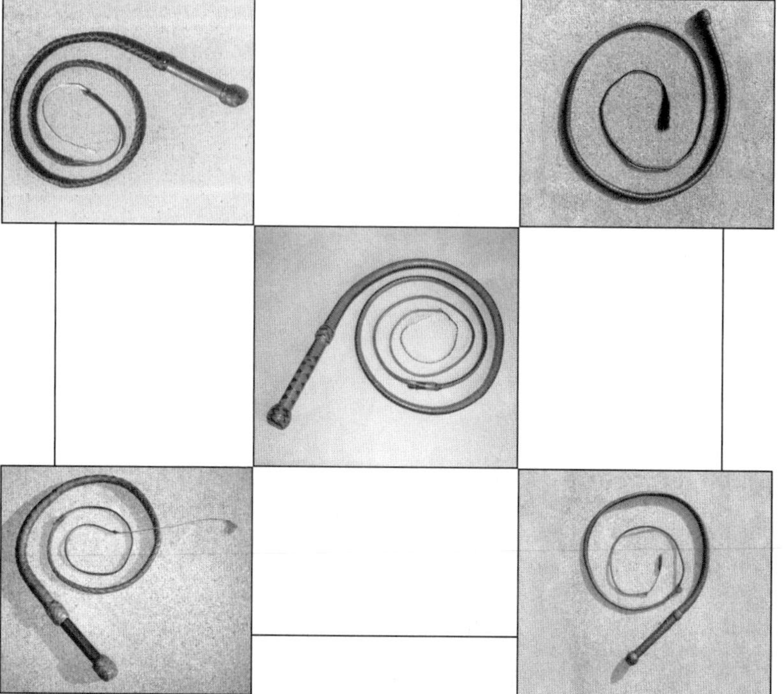

The Latigo y Daga Association

The Latigo y Daga Association is dedicated to the promotion of the whip and dagger arts found in the Filipino martial arts. Founded in 1987 by Tom Meadows, the association welcomes all practitioners and students of the martial arts. The whip is just one of the many flexible weapons found in the Filipino arts, and the purpose of the association is to provide information and training resources to all martial artists interested in experiencing the range and diversity of the Filipino martial arts.

The Latigo y Daga Association and its instructors can be contacted through its official Web site at www.latigoydaga.com.

LATIGO Y DAGA CERTIFIED INSTRUCTORS

There are currently six instructors certified to teach the Latigo y Daga system. They have each met the minimum requirement of 5 years of training with the whip and have a solid foundation in the basics of the system. Because of his own training background, each instructor has developed unique techniques for the whip, and cross training with more than one of these instructors is recommended and encouraged.

Mike Krivka

Mike Krivka is one of the founding members of the Latigo y Daga Association and has been training with the whip since 1990. Mike is the first instructor certified by the association and is the head instructor in the system. Mike has shown tremendous dedication to the art of the whip and dagger and has been instrumental in its technical development and growing recognition.

Tom Meadows and Mike Krivka.

Mike is the training director and head instructor of Martial Arts Koncepts and has been a student of the martial arts for a quarter of a century. He actively trains with Guro Dan Inosanto and is currently an associate instructor in Jun Fan Gung Fu/Jeet Kune Do Concepts, the Filipino martial arts of kali, eskrima, and arnis, as well as Maphilindo silat.

Mike Krivka and his Latigo y Daga students with Tom Meadows.

In addition to his extensive qualifications in law enforcement training, Mike is also certified to teach other arts, including JKD Unlimited and High Performance Martial Arts under the direction of Sifu Burton Richardson, Combat Submission Wrestling under the direction of Sensei Erik Paulson, and Lameco Eskrima under Punong Guro Edgar Sulite.

Jeff Finder

Jeff "Stickman" Finder has been training with the whip since his early childhood and joined the Latigo y Daga Association in 1993. Jeff has contributed much to the whip and dagger arts and the martial arts in general, which resulted in his induction into the U.S. Kali Association Hall of Fame.

Left to right: Jeff Finder, Tom Meadows, and Professor Ron Lew.

Jeff began his pursuit of the Filipino arts in 1979 and became a student of Angel Cabales' Serrada system in 1985. Jeff became a personal student and friend of Angel Cabales and trained extensively with him for several years. Cabales awarded Jeff his advanced certificate in 1987. A successful international full-contact eskrima fighter, Jeff was the first to manufacture synthetic sticks for eskrima practitioners. The quality and durability of these products have earned him the name "Stickman."

Ron Balicki

Ron Balicki brings to the Latigo y Daga system a blend of skills, real-world combative experience, and teaching ability that makes him a tremendous asset. Ron has supported the Latigo y Daga Association for many years and was directly involved in creating the terminology and framework used to teach its techniques.

Ron and his wife, Diana Lee Inosanto, are both active in the Screen Actors Guild and have numerous stunt and acting credits, and their Martial Arts Research system has a large international base of instructors and students. Ron has trained with Guro Dan Inosanto for 16 years and is one of the few Inosanto instructors to be certified in all three of the separate arts of Jun Fan gung fu, kali, and Maphilindo silat.

Ron is ranked as a senior assistant instructor under the late Punong Guro Edgar Sulite. Ron is also an instructor in Wing Chun under Sifu Randy Williams, an instructor in Muay Thai under Ajarn Chai Sirisute, and a third-degree black belt under Fred Degerberg. A very accomplished full-contact fighter, Ron has had several middleweight division professional fights in Japan. He holds the rank of shooter (professional fighter) under Sensei Yorinaga Nakamura.

Left to right: Anthony DeLongis, Ron Balicki, Tom Meadows, and Steve Kohn practicing on a rainy day in Los Angeles.

Steve Kohn on the receiving end of a combative technique by the author.

Steve Kohn

Steve Kohn has diligently pursued his personal study of the whip and has had the benefit of training directly with Tom Meadows, Ron Balicki, and Anthony DeLongis as individual instructors, as well as during their group training sessions. Steve traveled with Ron Balicki as his assistant for the latter's international seminar program and is certified under him as an associate instructor in both the Jun Fan martial arts and kali. This has given Steve a broad technical base to use in his own exploration that has resulted in some unique applications of the whip and dagger arts.

Steve is very fortunate to be thoroughly versed in both the DeLongis and the Latigo y Daga methods of whip manipulation. As a professional musician, Steve compares the two styles like this: "If what Anthony DeLongis does is jazz, then what Tom Meadows does is rock and roll."

Professor Ron Lew

Professor Ron Lew has more than 40 years of training in the martial arts and is the quintessential Tibetan arts teacher. In 1974 he founded the Tiger Eye Claw Center in San Jose, California, as a Tibetan arts center for the martial and healing arts. Professor Lew offers a full range of classes there, and Grandmaster Cacoy Canete uses this school as his regional training center.

Professor Lew has been fortunate to study forms under Kajukenbo grandmaster Ted Sotelo, and this study, along with many years of Chinese chain whip training, has had a profound influence on the quality of his whip work. Professor Lew's manipulations of the whip have a subtlety of grace and power that must be seen to be believed. These applications are visible manifestations of what is known as chi energy and are very rare in the whip world. Although the foundation of these techniques is rooted in the Latigo y Daga basics, they are distinct enough to warrant special classification. They have been formally recognized as unique to Professor Lew, and in 1999 he was authorized to create a subsystem of Latigo y Daga called the "Tibetan Wave." Professor Lew says of his Tibetan Wave whip techniques:

> Some of the basic Tibetan principles involved are yin/yang, playfulness, and interweaving the human spirit with the whip. There is the blending of the whip's motion, the human body, and the movements of the free hand. Fellow whip practitioners should practice softness of the fall and the motion of the thong. Study the entry and exit of the fall and take full advantage of the acceleration/deceleration of the thong. Be aware of your body's position in order to dance with the whip's motions of entry and exit. Be willing to explore the whip movement and body motions. Appreciate the fluidness and interconnection of the whip and you. The

Professor Lew demonstrates the "Tibetan Wave" technique called "Tiger goes down the mountain."

whip is alive; just as you are alive. Let the whip possess you, let it be creative, and let your inner child come out and PLAY.

Professor Lew's "Tibetan Wave" students at a seminar in San Jose, California, in 2004.

Anthony DeLongis

Anthony DeLongis is a professional actor, fight choreographer, and weapons specialist. This range of skills, which includes his whip work, makes him a tremendous asset to the Latigo y Daga instructors group. His personal style is highly fluid, and he has many years of serious research into proper whip use and training methods. His instructional methods reflect this research and allow him to develop top-grade whip skills in his students with the utmost efficiency. His experience with European sword and dagger work, in combination with his Filipino martial arts training, allows him to present the blade arts from a unique perspective and with the same quality of instruction found in his whip work.

Anthony works closely with his wife, Mary, who is also a talented whip artist. Together they perform in Wild West action shows, including horseback-mounted cowboy shooting and whip work.

The author and Anthony DeLongis.

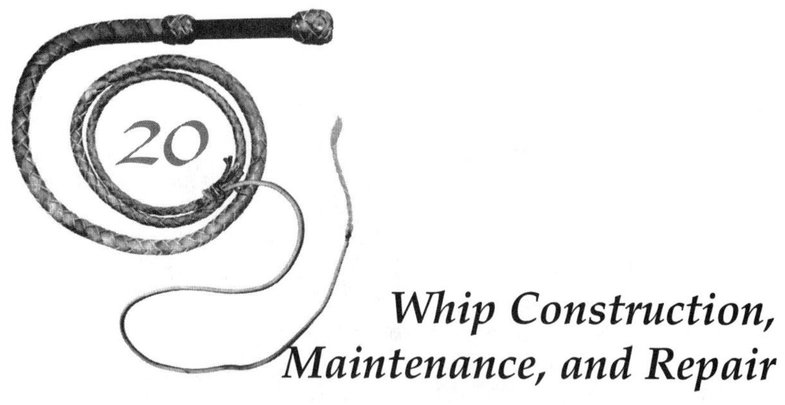

20 Whip Construction, Maintenance, and Repair

One of the most valuable resources for any whip user is his whip maker. A good whip maker is like the finest English tailor who carefully fits the product to the customer's individual needs. Like a good suit of clothes, a handmade whip will last a lifetime and tells the world much about its owner. As you work with your whip maker, you begin to trust in his experience and skill, and this trust will be rewarded with a tailored whip that feels like a natural extension of your body.

PETER JACK

Peter Jack is the premier New Zealand whip maker, whose whips have been described as "moving like water." His customers know Peter Jack as "the Whip Man," and for the past 20 years, his aim has been to revive the age-old craft of real whip making, which had all but died out in New Zealand. Peter Jack's self-defense whips are simply the best made and perfectly complement the combative perspective of the Latigo y Daga system.

Peter Jack in his workshop in New Zealand.

Peter offers a high-quality line of braided products, each made exclusively by Peter himself, and his kangaroo-hide whips are shipped with a tin of his whip wax and four spare crackers/poppers. Peter's whip wax is made from beeswax that he obtains from his own hives. This whip wax is the finest product of its kind on the market and is unsurpassed as a break-in wax. For regular maintenance, it holds up under the most demanding weather conditions and will preserve your whip for a lifetime of use.

Peter sells a complete range of custom-made poppers to meet specific needs, whether for cattle herding, precision cutting, or trick whip cracking. Peter also sells replacement falls handcrafted for different whip lengths and weights. Fall and popper replacement is part of the normal maintenance for the whip owner, and in the following photo sequences, Peter instructs you how to correctly replace the fall and popper.

These photos demonstrate how to replace the cracker on a whip.

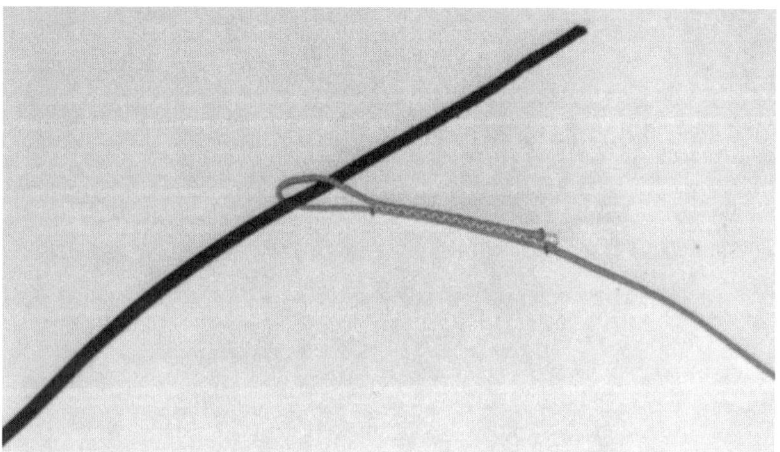

Thread the whip's fall through the loop of the cracker.

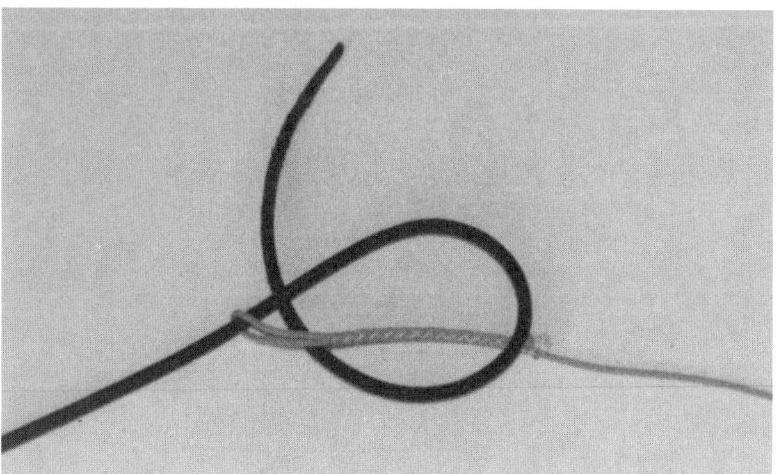

Loop the fall as shown.

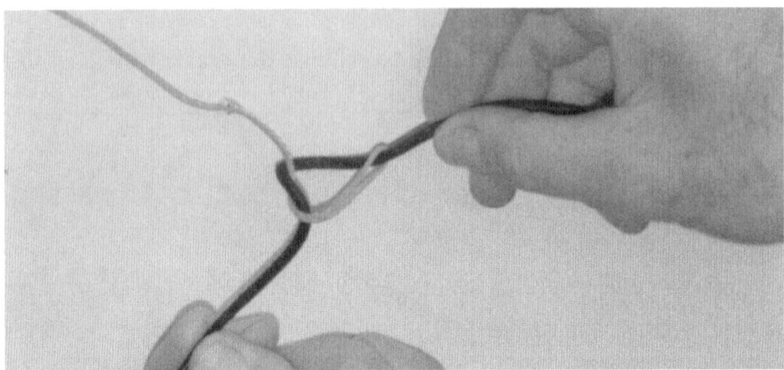

Pull the fall to straighten.

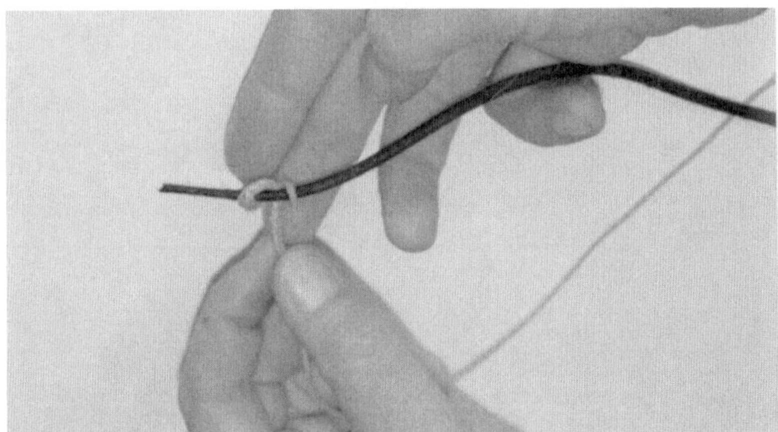

Move the cracker into position near the end of the fall and pull to tighten.

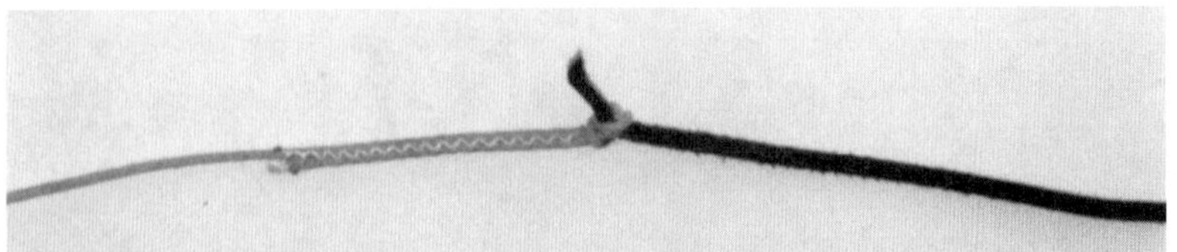

The tied cracker should look like this. NOTE: If the cracker slips off, rub the fall with methylated spirits (or denatured alcohol) before tying the cracker and then reapply a leather dressing.

These photos show how to replace the fall, or rat-tail.

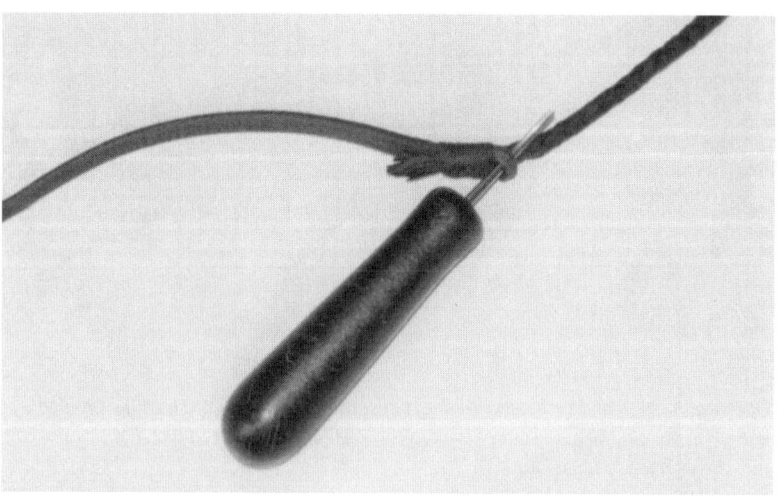

Thread a fid (or thick, blunt needle) through the top loop of the fall. This is visible at the top of the braided knot of the whip.

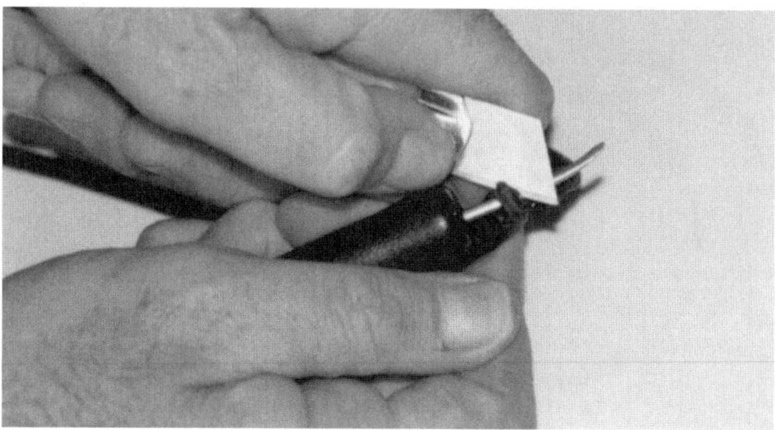

Cut through the fall loop with a sharp knife, being very careful not to cut any of the braided knot.

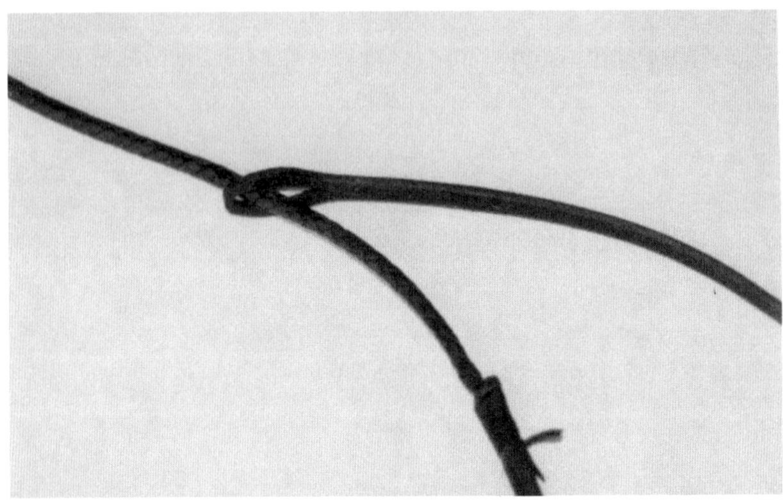

Open up the loop of a new fall and slide it over the old one right up past the braided knot. Pull the old fall down out of the braided knot and feed the thin end of the new one through the braided knot.

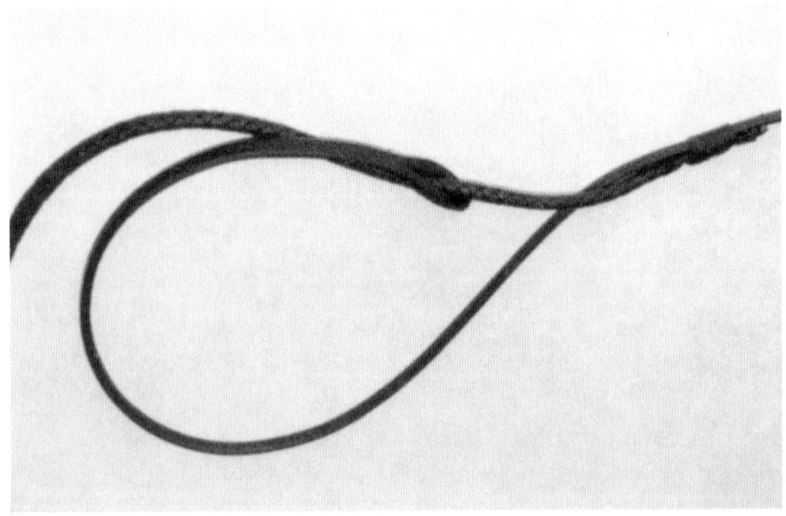

Pull the knot tight.

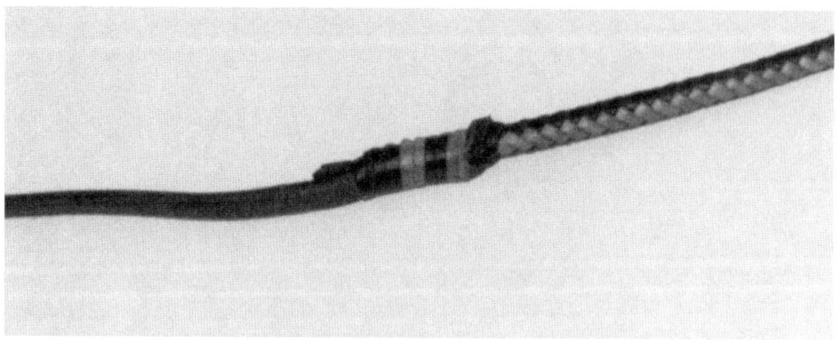

The replacement is complete!

Peter Jack, who lives in Timaru, New Zealand, can be contacted through his Web site (www.thewhipman.co.nz) for more information about his quality whips and leather products.

JOE STRAIN

Joe Strain is absolutely the best in the West! Joe's whips have been a tool of choice for Latigo y Daga students and instructors for quite a few years now. There are techniques within the system that were developed using his whips, and some of these have proven difficult to duplicate with other makers' whips. A Joe Strain whip will promote the effortless development of good whip technique and will give a lifetime of service as well.

Contact Joe at the following address:

Joe Strain
P.O. Box 1234
Rathdrum, ID 83858–1234
www.northernwhipco.com

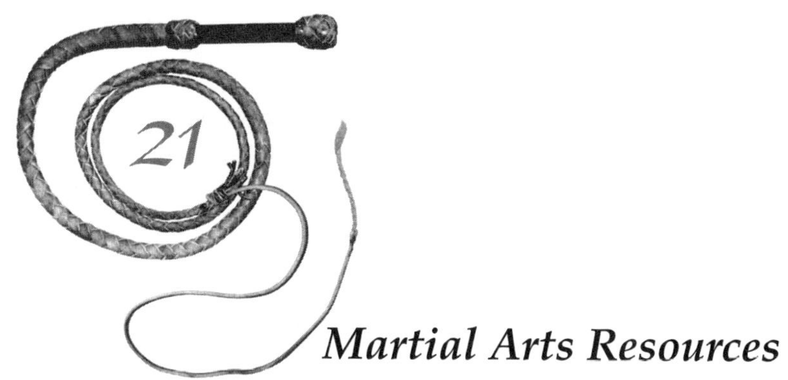

Martial Arts Resources

Anthony DeLongis, www.delongis.com
Anthony's homepage for his acting, stunt, and whip work, as well as broadsword and period rapier instructional videos. DeLongis is available for private lessons or group instruction.

Burton Richardson, www.jkdunlimited.com
Burton's Web site for his Jeet Kune Do training programs and more.

Cacoy Canete, www.cacoydocepares.com
Grandmaster Canete's Web site for his World Federation. This site maintains his list of certified instructors and his annual seminar schedule.

Doce Pares Eskrima, www.doceparesinternational.com
The official Web site for Doce Pares eskrima.

Dog Brothers Martial Arts, www.dogbrothers.com

The Dog Brothers motto says it all: "Higher consciousness through harder contact."

Grandmaster Amante P. Marinas Sr.

Grandmaster Marinas has an excellent line of instructional videos and books available on his Pananandata system. Pananandata books are available through www.paladin-press.com; Pananandata videos are available through www.espytv.com.

Guro Dan Inosanto, www.inosanto.com

Inosanto Academy of Martial Arts
13348-13352 Beach Avenue
Marina Del Rey, CA 90292

Herman Suwanda, www.suwandaacademy.com

The official Web site for Mande Muda Pencak Silat.

James Loriega, www.angelfire.com/ny/ninokai

The official homepage of the New York Ninpokai.

Lameco Eskrima, www.lamecoeskrima.com

The official homepage for Grandmaster Edgar Sulite's Lameco Eskrima.

Larry Hartsell, www.jkdassoc.com

The official homepage for Larry Hartsell's grappling association. Guro Hartsell is the premier Jeet Kune Do grappler in the world.

Marc "Animal" MacYoung, www.nononsenseselfdefense.com

The definitive Web site for street self-defense and related issues.

Martial Arts Koncepts, www.martialartskoncepts.com
Mike Krivka's martial arts Web site.

Martial Arts Research Systems, www.ronbalicki.com
The homepage for Ron Balicki's MARS organization.

Martin Seminars, Inc., www.martin-seminars.com
Martin Seminars organizes and coordinates seminars for top-ranked martial artists throughout the world and is affiliated with the Inosanto Academy and the Frances Fong Academy. Owner LaVonne Martin has instructor-level rank in eight different systems.

Michael DeVeny
Michael manufactures chain mail whips and custom chain mail goods. Contact him at the following address:
Michael DeVeny
5301 South Superstition Mountain Road
Suite 104 Box 119
Gold Canyon, AZ 85218

Mike Young, www.mdke.net
This Web page features videos of Guru Besar Herman Suwanda and is absolutely the best source for do-it-yourself training equipment.

Oakland Eskrima Club, http://members.aol.com/EKaliArnis/oec.html
Doce Pares instruction under Guro Reginald Burford in Oakland, California.

Pointman Productions, www.pointmanproductions.com
Books and videos for the martial artist produced by Ron Balicki.

Ron Lew, www.chi-energy.com
Professor Lew's Web site for Tibetan martial arts.

Stickman Products, www.stickman-escrima.com
Jeff Finder's homepage.

Tuhon Chris Sayoc, www.sayoc.com
The official Web site for Sayoc Family Kali.

Whipboxing, www.whipboxing.com
The Australians have formed a sanctioning organization to promote the art of sport whipfighting. Their approach to the many problems associated with safety and scoring shows much promise and opens up many possibilities for the whip arts.

Bibliography

The books and articles listed here were used as resource material for this book. They are all highly recommended reading for anyone interested in the whip and dagger arts.

Breen, Andrew. "Filipino Rope Technique." *Black Belt,* June 1992.

Canete, Ciriaco C. *Doce Pares*. Cebu, Philippines: Doce Pares Publishing House, 1989.

Draeger, Donn. *Weapons and Fighting Arts of the Indonesian Archipelago*. New York: Tuttle-Periplus Publishing, 2001.

Goriely, Alain, and Tyler McMillen. "The Shape of a Cracking Whip." *The American Physical Society,* Vol. 88, Number 24, June 17, 2002.

Inosanto, Dan. *The Filipino Martial Arts*. Los Angeles: KnowNow Publications, 1977.

Keating, James. "The Exotic Art of the Martial Whip." *Full Contact,* June 1994.

———. "The Martial Short Whip." *Full Contact,* August 1994.

———. "Whip It Out." *Full Contact,* June 1994.

Kier, Tom, and Jeff Chun. "The Combat Whip of Sayoc Kali." Internet article, www.sayoc.com, accessed 1999.

Loriega, James. *The Scourge of the Dark Continent: The Martial Use of the African Sjambok*. Port Townsend, WA: Loompanics Unlimited, 1999.

———. *Sevillian Steel*. Boulder, CO: Paladin Press, 1999.

Marinas, Amante "Mat" P. Sr. "The Philippine Latiko." *Black Belt,* March 1994.

Morgan, David. *Whips and Whip Making*. Centreville, MD: Cornell Maritime Press, 1972.

Sandburg, Carl. *Abraham Lincoln: The Prairie Years*. New York: Harcourt Brace and World, 1926.

Stewart, Oscar. *Physics*. New York: Ginn and Company, 1944.

Although not commercially available, technical articles written by Chris Smith and Anthony DeLongis were valuable contributions to the background material for this book.

Video Bibliography

Technical and textual material were also obtained from the following videotaped materials.

Allen, Mark. *Art of the Whip*. Oyster Bay, NY: Mark Allen Productions, no date.

———. *Whip Cracking Made Easy*. Netcong, NJ: Mark Allen Productions, 1992.

DeLongis, Anthony. *Mastering the Bullwhip, Vols. I and II.* Torrance, CA: Pointman Productions, 1998.

DeLongis, Anthony, and Colin Dangaard. *Whip Cracking with the Masters.* Malibu, CA: Australian Stocksaddle Company, 1990.

Jack, Peter. *The Ways of Whip: New Zealand Cracking Styles.* Timaru, New Zealand: Peter Jack, 1998.

Keating, James. *The Whip: Combat Applications*. Walla Walla, WA: ComTech Productions, 1994.

Sanchez, Snookie. *Whip Demonstrations*. Braulio Pedoy School, Hawaii. Courtesy of the Dog Brothers martial arts film library.

———. University of Hawaii, filmed by Michael Janich, 1994.
———. Black Belt Promotion Ceremonies in Hawaii, courtesy of Ron Tapec.
Woodward, Steven. *Mastering the Whip*. Orlando, FL: Black and Blue Productions, 1997.

Photo Credits

All photography by Tom Meadows unless otherwise indicated.

Photo of Momoy Canete provided by Richard Hudson.

Video footage of Snookie Sanchez provided by Michael Janich.

Photos with Guro Dan Inosanto Copyright IAMA 2004.

Photo of Tom Meadows and Frank Stearns by Frances Stearns.

Photo of Tom Meadows with Anthony DeLongis by Victor Gendrano/Pointman Productions.

Photo of Tom Meadows with Steve Kohn by Victor Gendrano/Pointman Productions.

Photo of Anthony DeLongis with dual whips by Victor

Gendrano/Pointman Productions.

Photo of Anthony DeLongis executing his signature loop provided by Anthony DeLongis.

Latiko technical sequence photos courtesy of Grandmaster Amante P. Marinas Sr.

Whip repair and maintenance photos courtesy of Peter Jack.

Photo of Mike Krivka and his students by Mykola Machnowsky.

Glossary

anting-anting: The application of spiritual powers to protect oneself in a fight. A fighter may also use another anting-anting practitioner to augment his own abilities in this area.

arnis: Baton-based Filipino fighting systems usually found in the northern portion of the Philippino archipelago.

bankaw: A long staff used for fighting.

baraw-kamut: The knife used in conjunction with empty-hand techniques.

bersilat: A Malaysian martial art similar to pentjak silat, which it is thought to have been derived from. Bersilat is a self-defense system dating from the 15th century with several styles, each with two branches, one for public display and one for combat.

bokken: A wooden Japanese fighting sword, usually made of oak. This type of sword is used in both training and actual combat.

carrenza: Free-form dances used to demonstrate the Filipino martial arts.

chemeti: An Indonesian ritual whip made of buffalo hide, human hair, or chain.

core: The internal portion of the whip that the outer layers are braided over. The most common core materials are leather, rope, and steel cable.

corto: This is the close range where the hands can touch the body and grappling techniques can be applied.

Doce Pares eskrima: A Cebuano style of eskrima founded by the Canete brothers in 1932. It is currently headed by Grandmaster Cacoy Canete.

dos manos: Two-handed techniques, either armed or unarmed.

dumog: A general term to describe Filipino wrestling and grappling.

escrima: A spelling variant of *eskrima*, referring to the baton-based Filipino fighting systems generally located in the central Philippines.

espada y daga: Techniques done with a sword in one hand and a dagger in the other.

fall: The fall attaches to the thong of the whip and is usually around 24 inches in length. It can vary in both thickness and length, and these variations are used as a means of fine-tuning the action of the whip.

grip: The external portion of the whip held by the user, usually defined as the area between the upper and lower knobs.

hampak-higot: Thrusting with the fingers.

hubad-lubad: Two-handed trapping and locking; to tie and untie.

internal handle: The internal stiffening rod that the grip is braided over. The rod is usually wood, steel, fiberglass, or aluminum and can vary significantly in length, depending on application.

Jeet Kune Do: Bruce Lee's analytical method for training and studying in the martial arts.

kali: This term usually refers to Filipino martial arts styles practiced by the Moros and other people based in the southern Philippines. This term is considered by some to be the oldest name for the various Filipino martial arts.

Kali Intra: The name of Maestro Snookie Sanchez's martial arts system.

kamut-kamut: The use of empty hands against empty hands.

kanggan: A Filipino jacket.

knob: This is a heavy, thick circular braid usually placed at the bottom of whip and also just above the grip area to keep the whip from coming out of the user's grasp.

kuntao: An aggressive, combat-oriented system of Chinese fighting arts as practiced in Indonesia and Malaysia.

kuntaw silat: A general term describing a blend of Chinese fighting arts and Indonesian silat techniques; also known as kuntao silat.

kuntaw: Filipino fighting arts developed by Muslims of the southern Philippines using a technical base from Chinese kuntao.

largo mano: Long-range stick techniques in which only the opponent's hands and stick are in striking range.

malong: A simple, tubular, highly functional piece of cloth worn by Muslims that is similar to a sarong in wear and combative application.

Maphilindo: A term used to describe the **Ma**laysian-**Phil**ippino-**Indo**nesian martial arts as a whole. It was coined before *Filipino* became more common than *Philippino*.

medio: This refers to the medium fighting range where both players' hands can reach each other's bodies but are not close enough to effectively engage in grappling.

olisi-baraw: Techniques done with a short weapon in one hand and a long weapon in the other; stick and dagger.

olisi-palad: Short pieces of rattan or hardwood approximately

5 inches in length that are held in the palm to reinforce striking techniques; palm sticks.

olisi-toyuk: Filipino rice flail with two short rattan sticks joined by a piece of cord. This can be used to remove the hulls from rice or as a weapon; similar to the Japanese nunchaku.

pana: Filipino bow and arrow.

Pananandata: A classical form of weapons defense taught by Grandmaster Amante P. Marinas Sr. This style encompasses a full range of weaponry including the latiko-style whip.

panatukan: Filipino boxing methods.

panu: A Filipino scarf or handkerchief.

Pekiti-Tirsia: The family kali system of the Tortal family. It is currently headed by Grand Tuhon Leo Tortal Gaje Jr.

Pencak Silat Mande Muda: This silat style was founded by master teacher Uyuh Suwanda in Bandung, West Java. This style was taught extensively in the United States by Guro Besar Herman Suwanda, now deceased, and is currently led by his daughter, Guro Besar Rita Suwanda.

pentjak silat: A general term referring to silat fighting systems found in Indonesia and Malaysia; also pencak silat.

petjat: The petjat is a type of whip used in the Indonesian udung whip system. The petjat is 4 to 6 feet in length and is made of strong, twisted, coconut-palm fibers.

pitik-pitik: To hit, tie and untie

plaits: The number of individual strands used to braid a whip, usually ranging from 4 to 24 in number. The use of more plaits generally results in a finer action and a higher-quality whip.

popper: A short piece of twisted string or similar material that attaches to the end of the fall. The popper is usually around 8 inches in length.

putong tagkus: A Filipino headband.

sabitan: A belt worn around the waist.

sarong: A tube of cloth that can be worn in many fashions around the body. Common to many island cultures and particularly Indonesia, where it is used as a weapon with other fighting techniques.

sayaw: Filipino prearranged forms for demonstrating martial technique by one or two persons or larger group.

Sayoc kali: The blade-based portion of Sayoc family fighting system. It is described as an "all blade—all the time system" by Tuhon Chris Sayoc, who is the fifth-generation system head.

Serrada escrima: Grandmaster Angel Cabales' close-quarter style of escrima that uses a short stick, typically from 18 to 24 inches in length.

sibat: An oar used for fighting.

sikaran: A method of Filipino foot fighting.

silat: A general term used to describe various fighting arts found in Malaysia and Indonesia.

sjambok: A rigid African whip approximately 4 feet in length, traditionally made of rolled rhinoceros hide.

songab: Filipino boxing; panatukan.

Tapado: The escrima system of G.M. Romeo Mamar Sr. that centers around the use of a long stick or tree branch.

telson: A hollow, poisonous final joint found on some crustaceans.

thong: The main body of the whip, excluding the handle, fall, and popper.

tiban: See udung.

tjambuk: A secret Indonesian whip fighting technique displayed only during a special folk dance.

udung: This is an Indonesian whip system that is principally ceremonial. Udung practitioners believe that the whip's action will produce needed rain. Also known as tiban.

About the Author

Tom Meadows began his study of the whip in 1957 when he was 5 years old. In 1962 he began his formal training in the martial arts with the study of archery and Kodokan judo in Tokyo, Japan. Twenty-five years later, in 1987, he began his training in the Filipino martial arts under Guro Dan Inosanto. Currently he holds instructorships under Guro Inosanto in the Filipino martial arts and the Jun Fan martial arts of Bruce Lee.

In 1988 Meadows began his study of Doce Pares eskrima under Skip Jordan in San Luis Obispo, California. He continued his Doce Pares training with Diony Canete and later as a personal student of Grandmaster Cacoy Canete, who is the current head of the Doce Pares system. Meadows holds a master's ranking under Grandmaster Canete in eskrima/eskrido and is a fourth-grade black belt in Grandmaster Canete's system of barehanded combat known as Pangamot.

In 1989, as a member of the 21-man U.S. full-contact eskrima team, Meadows went to Cebu City, Philippines, and won the superheavyweight world championship title at the first international eskrima, kali, and arnis championships. In the year 2000 he won the World Eskrima Arnis and Kali Federation U.S. Master's Forms championship using the whip and dagger.

Tom Meadows at the first international eskrima, kali, and arnis championships in Cebu City, Philippines.

With encouragement from his instructors to explore other arts, Meadows has also trained in Muay Thai kickboxing, Lucay-Lucay Kali, Indonesian silat, traditional wrestling, and Brazilian jiu-jitsu, and has earned belt ranks in aikido, aiki-jujitsu, judo, and savate.

As an author, Meadows has published feature articles in *Black Belt, Inside Kung Fu, Inside Karate,* and *Martial Arts Training.* He recently coauthored the biography of Grandmaster Cacoy Canete, which details many of the more than 100 challenge fights Canete fought during his lifetime.

Video footage of Tom Meadows' full-contact sparring with the whip, the baton, and the staff can be found on tapes one, two, and six of the *Real Contact Stickfighting* videotape series available through Panther Productions.

Tom Meadows lives in Cambria, California, where he teaches the Latigo y Daga whip and dagger system, Doce Pares eskrima, and Jun Fan/Jeet Kune Do concepts.